Inspiring | Educating | Creating | Entertaining

Brimming with creative inspiration, how-to projects, and useful information to enrich your everyday life, Quarto Knows is a favorite destination for those pursuing their interests and passions. Visit our site and dig deeper with our books into your area of interest: Quarto Creates, Quarto Cooks, Quarto Homes, Quarto Lives, Quarto Drives, Quarto Explores, Quarto Gifts, or Quarto Kids.

First Published in 2021 by Cool Springs Press,
an imprint of The Quarto Group,
100 Cummings Center, Suite 265-D, Beverly, MA 01915, USA.
T (978) 282-9590 • F (978) 283-2742 • QuartoKnows.com

Cool Springs Press titles are also available at discount for retail, wholesale, promotional, and bulk purchase. For details, contact the Special Sales Manager by email at specialsales@quarto.com or by mail at The Quarto Group, Attn: Special Sales Manager, 100 Cummings Center, Suite 265-D, Beverly, MA 01915, USA.

25 24 23 22 21    2 3 4 5

Print ISBN: 978-0-7603-6819-0
Digital edition published in 2021
eBook ISBN: 978-0-7603-6820-6

Library of Congress Cataloging-in-Publication Data available

Design and page layout: Laura Shaw Design, Inc.
Cover images: Kelly D. Norris
Photography: Kelly D. Norris; except Austin Eischeid, page 123; James Golden, pages 138–139, 150–151; Tony Spencer, page 83; Kristl Walek, page 198 (left); Scott Weber, pages 182 (right), 183; and Paul Westervelt, page 122

Printed in the USA

# NEW NATURALISM

Designing and Planting a
Resilient, Ecologically Vibrant
Home Garden

**KELLY D. NORRIS**

COOL
SPRINGS
PRESS

# CONTENTS

*The Beginning*   6

**Section 1**

## THE NATURE OF PLANTING

*About Plants and Place*   9

**CHAPTER 1**  Understanding Plants   10

**CHAPTER 2**  Understanding Places for Planting   34

**CHAPTER 3**  Techniques for Making Beautiful,
Ecologically Vibrant Gardens   54

**Section 2**

# PLANTING PALETTES

*A Few Words about the Palettes*   113

**CHAPTER 4**  Open Landscapes    114
**CHAPTER 5**  Planting Close to Home    138
**CHAPTER 6**  Softening the Hardscape    166
**CHAPTER 7**  Green Shade and Dappled Edges    186

*Conclusion: The Nature of Growing*    203

*About the Author*    204
*Index*    205

# THE BEGINNING

*First follow NATURE, and your judgment frame*
*By her just standard, which is still the same:*
*Unerring Nature, still divinely bright,*
*One clear, unchang'd, and universal light,*
*Life, force, and beauty, must to all impart,*
*At once the source, and end, and test of art.*

—ALEXANDER POPE, from "An Essay on Criticism"

**THE POET** Alexander Pope might have given the world the soundest gardening advice when he penned "First follow NATURE." Nature has had a seemingly uncomfortable association with gardening for centuries, even as gardeners have remained in earnest pursuit of *naturalistic* landscapes. It's a curious paradox. Traditional gardening, as practiced by self-espoused nature and outdoors lovers, has often led to strong preferences about the kinds of nature we welcome into the garden: butterflies are good but deer are bad. We've not followed nature as much as we've tried to lead it.

I didn't encounter Pope's words until my freshman year in college and didn't think much of it with respect to my gardening life until years later. When I did, I began to connect the dots. Around age 12, I professed a curiosity to explore a remnant, 40-acre tallgrass prairie next to my grandmother's farm, where I learned much about gardening against the backdrop of Iowa's agricultural countryside. Growing up nearby, the wild roadsides of my rural upbringing proffered introductions to some of my oldest gardening friends—*Aquilegia canadensis* (wild columbine) and *Tradescantia bracteata* (prairie spiderwort) are plants I still grow today. The neighborhood prairie might as well have been a botanical block party, even if it was only politely regarded by local farmers as a good source of late-season hay. Although I couldn't formulate the words for my feelings then, I realize that I was enchanted by observing plants in place, bearing witness to their wildness absent much in the way of human gestures. That prairie, which I fondly think of as my home prairie for all the good it did me growing up, was a harbinger of heritage and hope.

I got the chance to wander amid those tall stands of *Sorghastrum nutans* (Indiangrass) and occasional copses of *Amorpha fruticosa* (false indigo bush). In my wide-eyed pubescent years, I could have tracked my growth spurts standing tall against the gangly stems of *Baptisia alba* (white indigo). As a teenager, I came to know two federally threatened species that called that prairie home: *Asclepias meadii* (Mead's milkweed) and *Platanthera praeclara* (western prairie fringed orchid). Those chance encounters with botanical treasures rewired my view of the natural world, cultivating a fascination with plants and place. In college I delved into that fascination with plants, their biology and ecology, their cultivation as elements of designed landscapes. Much of my writing and communication in those years dealt with the palette with which gardeners plant and seek to inspire readers to explore plants as much as grow them for whatever purpose. A deep, abiding understanding of plants remains the most fundamental plank in my horticultural practice today.

Let's be clear—this book is not merely some prairie boy's plea to re-wild the planet, even if I entice your untamed notions. Wisecracking skeptics may deride the prairie as the poster child of wildness run astray with modern garden design. Perhaps it looks like that. For all the buzz about naturalistic planting, it's easy to think that the best way to make a wilder landscape, both for looks and cause, would be to order a packet of wildflower seeds and simply dash across a tightly clipped lawn flinging hope and aspirations in protest to that underfoot. The only thing I'll protest is treating plants merely as static, colorful furnishings in the outdoor room; plants are characters with stories to tell.

Planting on the wild side is hands-in-the-dirt activism, my favorite act of gardening, as transactionally important as weeding but so much more gratifying. While I find some therapy in the latter, I delight in few things as much as the seminal act of committing plants and seeds to the ground. Planting in this way sets in motion the stories of plants as characters within the place you call home. There's something magical and nearly alchemical about it all, a sort of wizardry that turns out right, even if it's not quite as you imagined it. I hope you might begin to see your garden beyond merely a resource-intensive, two-dimensional art form and instead, as a self-perpetuating, three-dimensional life form.

However, if you read this book thinking that I might pronounce in some masterly way all there is to know about planting wilder gardens, you'll be sorely disappointed. The book is not a profession of mastery, but rather the pursuit of it. I've attempted to chock it full of opportunities and insights with the ultimate realization that the story will continue to grow and unfold. In that way, writing this book is less about pronouncements and rules, dos and don'ts. My goal is to inspire you to achieve something beautiful and functional. Gardens can be both reservoirs of ecological goodness, even merely interventions with the wild, and beautiful works of art.

None of this means you'll need an ecology degree to make your way through the text. The book will demystify and unpack heady ecological concepts that will empower you to plant and experiment with confidence, all while appealing to a sense of style. I've tried to keep much of the book as accessible as possible, even as I often wanted to dive deeper and unravel more complexity. I have no plans to drone on about the usual talking points without giving them context, considering their applications to gardens or rebutting them altogether. Natural sciences are messy, particularly when applied to something equally as messy as a landscape dominated by humans. We are part of the natural equation, not removed from it, if only we'd acknowledge the opportunity to garden our backyards as slivers of the natural world. Think of all of this as an encouraging conversation between gardeners, if also occasional genial prodding. Through teaching and sharing these insights with diverse audiences over the last several years, I find that much of the science in the book comes alive with practice and observation and tends to reinforce things you might have already noticed while weeding. In reality, your garden is already closer to nature than you realize.

Recipes and good techniques matter. Just ask Julia Child. The masterwork that launched her fame effectively distilled the enormity of the French culinary genre into something demonstrable and achievable in the home kitchen. While the field of New Naturalism might not be as culturally integrated as a culinary tradition, its emergence as a nature-forward approach to making landscapes warrants some guide to help the everyday gardener make sense of it. This also provides the opportunity to redefine the culture in horticulture as a relationship *with* nature rather than a boundary between it. No gardener sets out to do wrong to the world by any act of gardening, but what if we were more conscious about doing right by it? This presents the need for clear, thoughtful strategies that might help us reprogram our plantings and subsequent gardening activities. The ideas here are meant to transcend climate, even if they require some generalization. The planting palettes that form the substance of this work are not meant to be comprehensive or all-inclusive; they even sometimes make egregious assumptions in hopes of conveying some example that you might plant and grow from.

Finally, this book will go to great lengths not to romanticize an array of honorable, worthy superstars for all their gleaming successes. Such an effort would seem to set the practice of naturalizing gardens atop lofty pedestals achieved only with credentials. This book is instead a primer for a better way, hewn from considerable study of plants and their ecology. Above all, I just want more people to plant on the wild side, to embrace the nature of gardens as they are and can be. I don't encourage rulers or grades to measure progress. We need millions of people planting differently for a planetary purpose, even if that's one thoughtful decision at a time.

# THE NATURE OF PLANTING

## About Plants and Place

History is full of great visions about landscapes that rest on the mantle of place. The Romans had a phrase —*genius loci*—that quite literally referred to the protective spirit of a place. American landscape architect Frederick Law Olmsted was often called a "genius of place," the literal translation of said phrase due to his uncanny ability to depict scenery in the most disarming and convincing ways. Yet for all this fascination with wild scenes and natural constructs, gardening is so often disconnected from nature's mechanics despite our most earnest convictions and intentions. Nature, if conceived as some mothering spirit, would seem to surround us anyway. Now, it's time to take notice.

The following chapters serve to illuminate our horticultural surroundings as mere inscriptions into a greater order; an intervention with place through plants. The next two chapters attempt to inspire more opportunities for listening, watching, and learning from our gardens as patches in nature's quilt. Chapter 1 delves into the biology and ecology of plants in the context of nature's operating systems. Plants interact with soils as opposed to merely relying on them for stationary support; below the surface there's far more to the story. Plants interact with each other above

ground, too, which begins to influence and inform planting choices in a completely different way than merely what looks good in companionship. Planting can still be beautiful and cathartic if not also applied with science that lessens the fussing and encourages the buzzing.

For all that's fascinating and insightful about plants as organisms, what's most important is how we apply that newfound understanding to the place we garden. Chapter 2 offers a template for how to perpetuate a nature-forward vision of landscapes that includes humanity as a player in place instead of a bumbling overlord. Rather than merely applying vision and ideas to the landscape, why not reveal the nature of one lurking under your feet if only you'd give it a frame or embrace the potential of its indigenous roots? At the end of it, you should begin to adjudicate planting decisions not simply on aesthetic features, but by how those plants fit the place in all its spirited dimensions. The palettes in the latter section of the book begin to give shape to your planting plans by considering the ecological realities of various zones of the landscape and how you might begin to cultivate plant communities everywhere you can sink a shovel.

The author's front-yard Meadow Nord, a 3,200-square-foot (300 m²) planting pictured here in its second growing season after establishment.

# 1  UNDERSTANDING PLANTS

**AT THE JUNCTURE** of horticulture and ecology, New Naturalism is a reconciliation less for virtue and more out of necessity. In light of climate change and the human influence on the planet, our gardens aren't merely personal inscriptions on Earth's crust, but rather, the way we might cultivate wildness, both for a spirited sense of place and for all the life it might hold. At first, this could seem like a fairy tale about an Eden of promises and dreams. In fact, it's merely a recalibration of what a garden is and how we keep it. Traditional horticulture of the last several hundred years in the Western world has grown from a superficial, if not agronomic, foundation. Through exacting cultivation, regimen, and protocols, gardeners can produce the biggest pumpkin, the greenest hedge, or the lushest florals akin to yields in a field of commodity crops. A single plant or an artistic idea dominates our focus at any one time. In this paradigm, plants exist somewhat statically as if they were furniture in a beautiful room. This beauty flourishes on account of a resource called "the gardener." Planting, fertilizing, weeding, pruning, cutting back or tying up, dividing,

and replanting sound like the seasonally ordered to-do lists that govern the lives of many gardeners, one plant at a time. It's farming on a smaller scale, regardless of the crop or whether we're feeding anyone. This human-derived and human-focused landscape comes at a considerable cost, paid in dollars, sweat, and tears.

But what if we changed the objective and the rules of the game? Instead of arriving at a finish line at the end of the growing season, what if the garden became a place where a nearly infinite number of life cycles took place season after season if we'd only begin with informed planting choices? More than a parade of flowers and fruits, a cadence of life drives the rhythm of the seasons. We needn't observe the rituals of specimen care quite so carefully. In this paradigm, our role is to manage resources and apply them thoughtfully towards something more than pretty. Planting is an act of commencement. Weeding, pruning, and cutting back are editorial gestures that adjudicate the trajectory of the garden. Fertilizing as we know it is largely unnecessary. This garden isn't a hungry cause that we must slave over or that requires constant life support. It pays dividends and grows capital through perpetuation and persistence. It's a system that sometimes requires optimization even as it's responsive to change or disturbance. This richly complex garden doesn't exclude or except beauty—it exudes it.

We have to cultivate wildness by first understanding the wild lives of plants, both as individuals and as related guilds that reflect the nature of place. The results can be curious, enchanting, and beautiful.

## PLANTS ARE UP TO SOMETHING

In order to cultivate this new paradigm, we need to understand the nature of plants and their relationships to one another and the environment. Even so, there's so much to know about them, more than I could possibly cram or synthesize into this chapter. But as a gardener, there are a few themes worth understanding on a deeper level, lest you keep beating your head against the ground in bewilderment at why nothing succeeds. As gardeners, we especially want to understand how plants grow, survive, thrive, and disperse.

### Soil Is Where It All Begins

Soil biology is complex, even as it supports the basis of life in gardens. Throughout the history of gardening, we've often understood that something needs to be done to soil in order to condition it for whatever we might try to grow. An entire body of prescriptive literature exists on soils in gardens, seemingly for the purpose of selling products and services that correct some kind of deficiency. These ideas of increased nutrient consumption and availability have agronomic fingerprints all over them, and rightly so given that food crops require harvesting, which removes most of the biomass those plants would naturally return to the soil. Resilient gardens, though, are not grown for a seasonally definitive yield. The results are plural, not singular, and pay dividends over many seasons. Knowing your soil and its fertility can unlock profound insights into the kinds of plantings that are possible and how they might succeed.

Soils vary across the globe due to differences in parent material, topography, and climate, largely determined by temperature and the availability and activity of water. The soils that support desert biomes could not, given prevailing climatic patterns, support the expansive continental woodlands of the Americas, Europe, and Asia. Climate impacts both the structure and texture of soils, minerality, and the availability of nutrients to support plant life. In today's world, soils also vary due to human influence. The soil profiles of

urban environments rarely bear any resemblance to those that would have existed there historically. Soil maps of urban areas rarely have much value due to the cosmopolitan nature of soils disturbed by development or imported from elsewhere to replace native soil that has been removed. As a gardener, this can be frustrating and blindsiding without any more intelligence beyond that which you can observe via a test hole. Even a small property might have soils that vary considerably, with compaction often occurring near homes in the wake of construction or from human habitation. Ditches and waterways along streets or associated with topography introduce different moisture regimes that require thoughtful planting. Trees or outbuildings can have outsized influences on soil moisture, depriving some areas of it altogether or creating a shaded, humid zone that does not permit them

(OPPOSITE PAGE) Plants as individuals and communities thrive based on adaptations to the environments in which they grow.

(RIGHT) Much like our diets, our gardens need more nitrogen-fixing legumes. With nearly thousands of species across the globe, practically every local flora contains suitable examples for planting in gardens. Whether an annual as in the case of *Chamaecrista fasciculata* (partridge pea) (shown) or a perennial, these plants supply modest to robust levels of nitrogen to the soil through symbiotic relationships with bacteria that their roots encase in nodules.

to dry out. It's for these myriad reasons that soils are both cursed and celebrated, sometimes on the same day in the same garden.

Knowing your soil requires intimate inspection and a reality check—soil is really the final word when it comes to determining the basis for plantings. The intimate inspection can happen empirically and experientially. A soil test can give you sound insights into mineral composition, pH, amount of organic matter present, its cation exchange capacity, and often finer scale analyses for specific minerals, density, and water-holding capacity. All these metrics are often accompanied by agronomically conceived advice, which, with the exception of traditional vegetable production (the closest most gardeners get to growing crops), is mostly irrelevant in the ecological context. In the end, soil can be amended, but even

this is only gestural. The overall soil profile, including the parent material that your present soil formed in is the long-term influencer of all landscape activity as it concerns vegetation. You can't amend your way out of this reality.

Soil is alive, literally teeming with tens of thousands of species of protozoa, bacteria, fungi, and viruses and often hundreds of species of arthropods, earthworms, and small mammals. This pantheon of diversity works as a cohort, converting organic matter and plant exudates into nutrients that support the food web. Plants imbibe these nutrients in ionic forms dissolved in water in the soil, sometimes in large quantities such as with nitrogen, phosphorus, potassium, calcium, sulfur, and magnesium. Other trace minerals such as iron, zinc, and manganese are consumed in much smaller quantities. These nutrients form the basis of

## Healthy Plantings Aboveground Can't Exist without Healthy Soil Life Belowground

All this abridged soil science underscores that a designed, functional ecological landscape requires functional soil ecology. Some of these insights come from studying what you already have and understanding where your garden intersects and interacts with existing conditions. The ecologically driven approach to cultivating dynamic soil ecologies is less prescriptive and more facilitative.

**Reduce compaction.** By preserving and enhancing soil structure, you support the movement of air and water through the soil, which saves future plant life from the underground equivalent of a vice grip. Compacted sites don't exactly preclude plant growth, but plants establish and persist at a far slower rate. The severity and magnitude of compaction varies by soil type, so knowing what you start with forms the basis for how you manage it. Clay soils compact easily, reducing oxygen that's critical for supporting plant roots and the flow of nutrients through the soil.

**Enhance biological activity of the soil.** Recent research demonstrates that the most persistent forms of soil carbon come from dead microbes that have fed and completed their life cycle on plant-based tissues. Allowing surface organic matter to remain in the garden and decompose over time not only cultivates a vast herd of microorganisms stirring underneath but also buffers and protects soil from erosion and sequesters carbon (often more than plants and the atmosphere combined). Some plantings benefit from the addition of organic matter such as compost to ease the transition of new plants from the nursery container to the garden, acting as a bridge for young, developing root systems.

plant cells and tissues, the microscopic components of biomass.

Plants have also coevolved biochemical, mutually beneficial partnerships with this soil web to access soil nutrients. Plants exude sugars that feed these microscopic films of bacteria and fungi. These mutualisms are present throughout the plant world, but perhaps classically described in legumes and orchids. Arbuscular mycorrhizas, a gregarious class of root-penetrating fungi that associate with over 80 percent of all plant species on the planet, are the poster children for these symbioses. They forge dense networks through the soil that mitigate erosion and nutrient leaching, condition plants to drought stress by increasing water intake, help young plants establish by increasing root biomass, and bolster immunity against soil-borne pathogens. Protozoa, the bacteria-grazing unicellular microbes, are also titans of this underworld, generating nitrogen as waste, which in turn accounts for the majority of nitrogen used by plants. When the diversity of these otherwise ubiquitous microorganisms is impoverished, ecosystem function declines.

While many other books describe these complex processes in greater detail, the summative notion for creating dynamic plantings boils down to preserving the soil's capacity for cycling nutrients and for retaining those nutrients for use by plants in the garden instead of succumbing to runoff or erosion. By feeding the soil's living community with the residues our gardens already produce, we can keep nutrients flowing through our highly local systems and avoid the consequences of excess nutrient runoff with rampant fertilizer use. This idea will come around again in chapter 3 in a discussion of best practices for cutting back plantings ahead of a new growing season. It's fair to say there's more to soil than simply the numbers to denote pH, nutrient levels, and percentage of organic matter.

### Soils impact how much and how fast plants can grow

The rate at which plants generate biomass is called "productivity," and it factors enormously into the visual and ecological results for plantings over time. Think of

In a wetland, life depends on keeping up with your neighbors. The visual evenness of this abundant plant community reveals intense competition for relatively few niches.

Superbloom events in stress-prevalent ecosystems happen when increased rainfall results in large numbers of seedlings recruited from the seedbank to flower in one dramatic moment. Pictured here is *Heterotheca villosa* (hairy false goldenaster).

productivity as the ability of a plant to convert energy from the soil and the sun into an engine for surviving and reproducing. In horticulture, productivity is traditionally only discussed as a topic relative to producing crops, particularly when yields are the chief concern. If you're trying to grow the biggest tomatoes or champion pumpkins, you want highly fertile soils that result in plant productivity. But if you're trying to create resilient, diverse plantings, productivity isn't exactly an asset. Instead of a monoculture, the ecological garden is a dizzying polyculture with many components competing with one another and the environment. Productivity benefits some players at the expense of others, specifically those plants that can leverage soil fertility into biomass (think big leaves, dense stems, deep taproots). In the early years of a planting, the success of some species might be a misleading indicator of success if and when it starts to decline in diversity over time. Many failed plantings were the results of poor matches between site and palette before any other gardening sins were committed. Fertility is indiscriminate; a rich and fertile soil gives rise to all plants, the ones you want and the ones you don't.

Productivity is a function of the resources available for the growth and proliferation of plant biomass, but it hangs in the balance with stressors present in every ecosystem such as those imposed by climate.

Environments with greater productivity and minimal stress tend to feature plants with aggressive, colonizing habits that succeed by competing at size and scale, which leads to one or a handful of plants dominating the site and reducing diversity. These situations rarely feature annual plants, unless they're of weedier persuasions and tend to occur only in advance of the domination of longer-lived perennials. Consider riverine floodplains with lush, endless expanses of *Typha* spp. (cattails) or *Juncus*, *Phragmites*, *Phalaris*, *Cyperus*, etc. (rushes and reeds). In rich, fertile soils, competition exerts a strong force on the visual result of the community because of the ability of a few plants to dominate and succeed.

Conversely, environments with reduced productivity and greater amounts of stress tend to feature greater levels of plant diversity because less competition occurs between species, producing a more even visual effect. In essence, the stress from a lack of soil fertility levels the playing field, allowing more species to populate an area because any single species lacks the ability to outcompete its neighbor. Under these circumstances, perennial plants tend to occur as isolated individuals or in small patches with slow-growing, clump-forming architectures. Annual species can be abundant, often in response to favorable growing conditions at abbreviated times of the year. Think of the "superblooms" of

North American deserts and steppes or the South African Great Karoo—these florally intense displays feature a rich assortment of species comingling to great effect because and despite of extended periods of drought and low soil fertility.

### Plant architecture reflects adaptation to environment.

As plants evolved in different environments across the planet, they adapted to soils and climate with a striking diversity of botanical features that range from elegant to peculiar. Plant architecture—the growth habits of a plant as described by the arrangements of and relationships between leaves, stems, and roots—has major implications for gardening, the useful sort of insights that help you plant the puzzle. While the architecture described in the following has a strong basis in botany, what to do with them depends on their worthiness as a function of their role in garden ecology. These natural structures become building blocks for horticultural integrity and art.

At a basic anatomical level, plants produce biomass in two departments, one aboveground and the other belowground. Roots can account for between 20 to 60 percent of the biomass of a plant and provide the foundation for a plant's ability to anchor itself to soil (or to other plants in the case of epiphytes) and extract water and nutrients from that substrate. Add up one plant growing next to another and the array of interactions expands dramatically—plants in communities can complement, facilitate, and compete with one another, sometimes simultaneously within the lifespan of any individual plant. In ecosystems, plants are part of the biodynamic infrastructure, pipelines for organic compounds and water in and out of soil. The physical and mechanical qualities of roots, whether near the surface or deep in the ground, allow them to contribute to the formation and regeneration of soils.

But as important as roots are, they aren't seen in plantings. We have to calibrate the importance of having diverse root infrastructures with aboveground architecture based on the general shapes and forms of plants, which sheds insights on how and where

they want to grow. These architectural categories exist for all forms of plant life. Landscape architects often describe tree and shrub canopies by their shape based on whether they are pyramidal, rounded, columnar, layered, weeping, or shrubby. As helpful as that is aesthetically, it masks the ecological profiles of trees. Some trees are single trunked, solitary, and without the ability to regenerate like many conifers such as *Picea* (spruce), *Pseudotsuga* (fir), and *Pinus* (pine). Some trees, such as many species of *Acer* (maple) and *Cotinus* (smoketree), can withstand severance of their trunk, regenerating with an abundance of juvenile growth sometimes called watersprouts or suckers. The pruning traditions of pollarding and coppicing rely on this regenerative capacity to manage the size of certain species in landscapes. Some woody plants blur the distinctions between tree and shrubs with their ability to sucker and form large colonies such as *Amorpha* (false indigo) and *Rhus* (sumac). Applying this architectural understanding from an ecological perspective is more insightful because the way in

(OPPOSITE PAGE) Some pines withstand fire better than others, but even the most flameproof will succumb under the right conditions. Individual trees in this population of *Pinus ponderosa* (blackjack pine) lack the physiological capacity to regenerate, although seedlings will likely recolonize in time.

(RIGHT) This young stand of *Rhus copallinum* var. *latifolia* 'Morton' (Prairie Flame™ shining sumac) forms a shrubby copse as a result of biennial coppicing in order to preserve a somewhat open canopy and allow light to penetrate into the understory of the planting.

which a tree grows over time will exert considerable influence on the planting around it, even if you really admire the shape of its canopy.

Perennials can also be intuitively categorized by basic shapes (groundcovering, upright and rounded, reverse pyramidal, upright, or caespitose), but perhaps more informatively by how they persist from one season to the next. Some perennials do not die down in winter such as *Lavandula* (lavender) or *Phlox subulata* (creeping phlox) and maintain buds at the base of these stems above the ground. Some perennials die down and overwinter at ground level with crowns or rhizomes such as *Symphyotrichum* (asters) and *Hemerocallis* (daylily). Some perennials retreat completely to the ground, overwintering as bulbs, corms, or tubers such as *Lilium* (lily), *Crocosmia*, and *Dahlia*, respectively. Each of these strategies has some implication for relating plants to place but also for relating plants to one another. Not every plant will fit into these categories discretely, but take note of these growth habits as essential information for understanding plants in the garden.

How a plant persists also gives some clue for how long it persists, an insight of practical value to gardeners. Information regarding the lifespan of trees and shrubs is readily available for commonly offered species. Some trees attain ancient, noble proportions (such as *Quercus* (oaks) and *Ulmus* (elms) while others live fast and die young (such as *Populus* (poplars) and *Salix* (willows). Longevity in perennial plants is relatively unquantified and can sometimes vary greatly in different climates. As a gardener, it's easy to start noticing the plants that seem to hang around for years versus the ones that come and go. Think of *Paeonia* (peony), *Osmunda regalis* (royal fern), and *Baptisia* (wild indigo), which can live for decades without much care. These all have very persistent crowns or rootstocks that store reserves, providing them with some biological insurance policy. On the other end of the spectrum are *Echinacea* (coneflowers), *Digitalis* (foxglove), and *Verbascum* (mullein), which can persist in gardens for many years but often only due to reseeding as individual plants survive for only a few

## Quick Guide to Plant Architecture

There are inarguable correlations between plant architecture and the ecological niches plants occupy in the wild, which offer invaluable insights into how to grow them in gardens. Here, I've offered a synthesis of common features and corollary functions that you can observe and from which you can infer. Contrasting plant architectures becomes fundamental to assembling beautiful and resilient plant communities (see chapter 3). These ideas also permeate the latter half of the book in the presentation of planting palettes.

(TOP LEFT) **Ground-covering mats** include plants with ground-level stems or roots such as *Antennaria* (pussytoes) that form fine carpets of conservative foliage early in the growing season. This growth habit will sometimes smother plants that have relatively shallow root systems or small crowns at the soil's surface by outcompeting them for the same niche.

(ABOVE) **Erect, upright stems** are easy enough to picture for woody plants in the form of trunks, but even ferns like this *Polystichum munitum* (western sword fern) have ascendant or sometimes decumbent (growing at the surface) stems that increase in girth with the accumulation of leaves from prior seasons. Once the leaves reach a certain point in their development, they begin to arch over.

(BOTTOM LEFT) Plants that grow from **basal rosettes** support multiple leaves from a central, compressed modified stem and often flower on leafless spikes, which adds a bonus dimension for relating these plants to others. *Agave* (*A. schidigera*, shown) and *Taraxacum* (dandelions) are classic examples.

Many grasses and grasslike plants such as *Carex flagellifera* (weeping brown sedge) grow from **caespitose clumps** with upward growth emanating from a central point. Clump architectures can vary from rigid and upright to broad and spreading. Species with this architecture can be long-lived, competitive, and have some ability to withstand stress.

Some plants feature **emergent stems** with leaves that cover them along their axis, an admittedly loose descriptor for a vast array of plants. At almost 5 feet (1.5 m) tall, *Echinops ritro* 'Veitch's Blue' (Veitch's Blue globe thistle) forms a dense canopy of leaves along gray stems.

Plants that grow in **leafy mounds** like many species of *Geranium* (*G.* × *oxonianum*, pictured) typically have an infiltrating personality, competing in dense vegetation by emerging from a ground-level crown with weak stems and varying degrees of leafiness.

Other plants have **emergent stems** with predominantly basal leaves, at least at the beginning of the growing season, and nearly leafless, late-season flowering stems such as this *Symphyotrichum oolentangiense* (azure aster).

years. These plants tend to have shallow, fibrous roots and small crowns at or just below ground level. Annual plants are similar, rarely investing in extensive root structures when their primary programming directs them to flower and set seed.

Understanding longevity helps you understand how long plants persist in landscapes, even if you know them to be perennial. Other references offer insights into longevity by species at a regional level even as the topic remains poorly studied. My goal is simply to underscore that wild plant communities often contain species with multiple life histories, a valuable lesson worth applying in the garden. It's important to design plant communities with multiple life histories to ensure that there are always plants being recruited for open niches as other plants progress through their life cycles. With annuals, there's value in short-term affairs so long as their role is understood in the context of the planting. Conversely, trees and some ferns may outlive us if left to persist for decades. Life history, though, is only one dimension of a plant's success in your garden.

### There's more to plant survival than winter hardiness

Where or not a plant can simply survive seems like the barest, most minimum threshold for plant selection. By that definition, survival might count as simply making it through the first winter. What if, instead, we understood how plants thrive by achieving an optimum level of performance within a set of garden conditions? Enough with hoping and planting. Making a garden deserves more confidence, which requires more information.

Every garden is different, and how plants, even of the same species, perform under relatively common conditions can vary dramatically, sometimes to a gardener's consternation. Plant hardiness is often one of the democratizing metrics used to select plants for gardens. While you might be able to rattle off your winter hardiness zone with glib confidence, understanding plants requires knowing more than simply how cold it gets for one night (on average) from one winter to the next.

Beyond annual winter minimum temperatures, a litany of factors affects plant performance in the garden, so much so that any careful reading of horticultural science will soon underscore what gardeners often know from trial and tribulation—gardening is local and site-specific. But a quick list of prevailing factors, aside from cold or heat, would seem to have as much influence on a plant's survival including wind, annual amounts and forms of precipitation, summer humidity, drought tolerance, and the plant's ability to adapt and establish after planting or benign neglect. Even within a geographic region, subtle microclimates or local variations as a result of altitude, exposure, topography, and nature landforms can have outsized effects on which plants persist and for how long. I find most gardeners quickly become walking guidebooks to these details after just a few seasons, witnessing the direct implications of the environment on the plants we tend.

Taken together, plants survive at the intersection of productivity, as described previously, and stability, the relative ecological evenness of any ecosystem. British plant ecologist J. Philip Grime proposed a now widely regarded theory for understanding plant survival that has direct and relevant applications to social, communal plantings. According to Grime, plants function in their environments by virtue of being able to compete for resources (**competitors**), withstand environmental stress (**stress tolerators**), or thrive in the face of disturbance (**ruderals**). He posited his theory in pyramid fashion, sort of like the familiar soil triangle—plants function as a result of the cumulative importance of each of these three strategies, admittedly to varying degrees.

**Competitiveness** is informed by a plant's biology and life history, but chiefly results in the suppression of other plants in the community based on the resources available to do so. Hypothetically, when two species compete for identical resources in a stable environment, one will eventually drive out or suppress the other. In both the wild and the garden, competition isn't fair or equitable, asymmetrically favoring those plants that have an ability to persist on a lower level of resources or quickly convert soil fertility into biomass.

*Andropogon gerardii* (big bluestem) lives up to its name with extensive root systems and dense crowns that give it a competitive advantage in North American grasslands.

Competition affects plant populations but acts on individuals in close proximity. In the wild, competitors often grow big and tall and tend to thrive in relatively stable, productive conditions (i.e., greater rainfall and soil fertility) that promote biomass production. The tall grasses of the North American prairies—*Andropogon gerardii* (big bluestem) and *Sorghastrum nutans* (Indiangrass)—are classic competitors as are notorious garden rebels such as the Asian *Petasites* (butterbur) and the fast-growing *Paulownia tomentosa* (princess tree). The size and perennial longevity of each of these plants allow them to maintain a competitive edge in the accrual of environmental resources. They often have colonial tendencies, spreading by stolons or rhizomes. You should account for competitive tendencies when designing plantings, as this functional strategy can lead to horticultural chaos in the productive growing conditions of many gardens.

**Stress tolerators** survive in the face of environmental onslaughts such as rapid temperature fluctuations and low water availability by investing in organs that allow them to store resources and recover from stress quickly. They often grow conservatively, reaching reproductive maturity after extended juvenile periods and can remain small for much of their life. Alpine flora such as *Gentiana acaulis* (stemless gentian)

are classic stress tolerators, as are herbaceous plants growing in glades, natural crevices such as *Tetraneuris acaulis* (stemless four-nerve daisy), or other rocky environments such as the coastal, rock-dwelling *Crambe maritima* (sea kale). Stress-tolerant plants offer clues to their ability to thrive with unique storage organs such as caudices, deep taproots, or fleshy, succulent leaves. While stressful circumstances present themselves in the landscape or might even be desirable in the case of a rock garden, the principle of stress is one with which we should become more comfortable applying to horticulture. Stress tolerators and the communities they form in the wild are often some of the most biologically diverse and species rich—in short, stress is a good thing.

**Ruderals** are opportunistic plants that seize the moment, often in the face of disturbance such as changes to the amount of light available or physical perturbation to the soil itself. Think of opportunists as those that invest less in individual plants and more in copious amounts of seed. Many weeds have ruderal profiles, are often annuals, and produce plenty of seed that can proliferate should favorable conditions persist. Many of our beloved garden flowers such as *Cosmos bipinnatus* (garden cosmos), *Centaurea cyanus* (bachelor's buttons), and *Consolida regalis* (larkspur) are classic ruderals. Short-lived perennials such as

(RIGHT) *Aquilegia* hybrids (columbines) reseed readily in gardens even as individual plants live for only a few seasons.

(BOTTOM) This meadow at the edge of a northern temperate forest reveals how a diverse assortment of plants colonizes and populates all of the niches available in an ecosystem from the canopy to the understory.

## How Plants Metabolize Indicates Where They Are Best Adapted to Grow

In the unfolding story of why some plants live where they do, it's worth looking at how plant metabolism reflects the nature of place. Photosynthesis is the primary process through which plants convert sunlight energy in conjunction with carbon dioxide and water into carbohydrates and oxygen. Over 90 percent of plant species utilize the C3 pathway that is optimized for temperatures between 50 to 70 degrees Fahrenheit (10 to 21 degrees Celsius). Plants that utilize the C3 pathway tend to exist in temperate climates with moderate light intensity, moderate temperatures, and abundant moisture. In contrast, the 5 percent or so of plant species that utilize the C4 pathway evolved to thrive in areas with intense sunlight, intense temperatures, and often severe seasonal variations in moisture. That many grasses are C4 plants begins to explain their prevalence in midcontinental climates with hot, humid summers. The remaining handful of plant species, principally succulents, cacti, and some aquatic plants, possess Crassulacean acid metabolism (CAM) as an adaptive strategy to endure severe ecological stress, like that found in deserts. A majority of succulents occur in deserts, biomes often characterized by hot daytime temperatures and significantly cooler nighttime temperatures. While these descriptions are generalities, it helps to know that plants' connections to place come with hardwired, physiological adaptations. Gardening in the era of climate change will require us to think about how to bridge and adapt adjacent floras from climatic regions with physiologically relatable floras.

*Aquilegia* (columbine) and *Echinacea purpurea* (purple coneflower) also have opportunistic tendencies, persisting in the seed bank in gardens for many years, even as individual plants fade from memory. Reseeding is a good thing, even if it challenges the tidiest of gardening norms. Growing opportunists is essential to creating a kind of ecological insurance policy, as gardening is full of all kinds of disturbance, much of which we render on an annual or seasonal basis by tilling, weeding, fertilizing, or fussing. Forgive the wanderers—these seedlings simply grew from opportunity and something other than a weed should fill the gaps, after all. Growing a garden of *only* opportunists makes less sense, of course, despite the fact that the most popular garden plants (especially those used for bedding) have more ruderal tendencies than we'd care to admit. Such a garden isn't entirely without virtue, though, particularly if replanting them yearly isn't a resource-intense circumstance. Annual flowers are full of ecological value, often supporting multiple life stages of invertebrates within a single growing season.

In reality, almost all plants have some slice of each of these functional strategies—few species are purely competitive or purely opportunistic in the extreme. Rather, the mix of adaptive strategies amounts to an individual species' ability to coexist with others in a common situation. In a wild-occurring plant community, individual plants of different species have reached some equilibrium that reduces the amount of competition between them in contrast to higher levels of competition among them. Viewed another way, any given plant (Species A) in a wild community is likely competing more with other individuals of Species A than with Species B, C, or D. Of course, all of this makes sense when considering plants from a textbook perspective. But what happens visually and aesthetically when plant sociality ends up on the end of a trowel? Chapter 3 will explore how to apply these insights to three layers that form the initial structure of the planting.

## The Social Lives of Plants

At this juncture, understanding the social lives of plants becomes fundamental for good gardening. Like navigating a new social network of friends or colleagues, the more you can understand the way plants associate in your garden, the more effective your relationships with them will be. Trying to constantly coax an introvert out to a party doesn't make a lot of sense, nor does forcing an extrovert to stay isolated from the crowd. Despite anthropomorphic liberties, plants very much grow the same way as determined by their abilities to compete or tolerate stress and disturbance as just described. The more you get to know plants, the more you realize how capricious and dynamic they are in response to the environment around them. While this response may happen individually, the cumulative effects are observed at the landscape level. This is a good reminder that nothing in the garden stays the same for very long. Trying to cultivate stasis only works against the natural order.

### In the wild, plants grow in populations of related individuals

The idea of a plant population might sound foreign or even intimidating. In traditional gardens, particularly small ones, we might grow one or a couple individuals of any one plant. A population seems to imply a lot of one thing, and who has room for that? But even in ecology, population is a vaguely contextual term with regard to size. What a population does, though, is foundational to building a resilient garden. In the wild, plant populations exchange genes, compete for space, and represent multiple generations in the same place at the same time. These inherent workings are the sort of self-managing properties that plants as isolated individuals in traditional landscapes don't have. When one or a few plants die, it's a major event, often leaving a gap that nature finds a way to fill if we don't get around to it. Nature tolerates no vacancies.

In the wild, plant populations change over time in response to the environment and interactions among plants. The distributions of plant populations begin to form observable patterns across the landscape as a result of these changes. German horticulturists Richard Hansen and Friedrich Stahl spent decades in the mid-20th century studying perennials and published a masterful tome of insights called *Perennials and Their Garden Habitats* (North American ed., 1993). In that book, they described a scale of plant sociability from almost solitary to extensive colonies. These patterns build on the architectural and survival strategies discussed earlier, though the observations are always in context. While a given species generally has a consistent architectural form, the influence of the local ecology can affect how they proliferate and behave. You can probably think of plants that have "taken over" or that you wish would spread more. Taking a cue from the nature of plants will lead to more resilient results as opposed to some arbitrary arrangement based purely on how plants look next to one another.

Plants that grow as segregated, single individuals or in small clusters often are strict clumpers or have small rhizomes or stolons that spread only weakly. In the wild, such arrangements can suggest long-lived plants that invest in durable, persistent roots or that germinate conservatively. It can also suggest that a species is popular with herbivores, which limits its proliferation. Plants that grow in larger clusters of 5 to 10 plants often compete more vigorously, but they may not spread further due to limitations in the environment, pest pressures, or a general decline as they approach the end of their lifespan. Plants in the middle of the spectrum that form more aggregate patches with upward of 20 or more individuals often do so in response to favorable conditions in the environment and their ability to outcompete most plants nearby or spread to cover larger areas. Plants that form extensive colonies over large areas often have a dominant, excluding capacity; a greater ability to endure stress; or regenerate quickly after disturbance. Each of these ideas informs the planting palettes in the latter half of this book.

(TOP) Species of *Delphinium* such as *D. tricorne* (dwarf larkspur) tend to occur in wild populations as scattered individuals, even though the sum of the population is dazzling cobalt sprinkles through low grasses.

(LEFT) *Liatris spicata* (dense blazing star), a deeply rooted clumper, can form large patches of up to 20 individuals via reseeding.

## Plant populations relate to one another in communities under similar conditions that form patterns given time and space

If plants are individually up to something, what happens when groups of them get together in some kind of horticulturally contrived social situation? What follows could read like a character list from a sitcom. Imagine the vocal and gregarious one, the center of attention who's loud and boisterous and maybe even overbearing. Think then of the proverbial wallflower, withering in the face of too much attention. There are probably at least a few characters in between, mixing and mingling without causing too much trouble. They are affable, charming, or maybe just blandly inoffensive. While this metaphor borrows a little imagination, it's not hard to extend these profiles to the plants in our gardens. There are plants that spread, aggressively and often vegetatively. There are those that need constant coddling or pampering, perhaps because they grow too slowly or have exacting cultural needs. Some plants seem to get along just fine wherever you put them. Each of these observations is rooted in an ecological reality. Regardless of the setting or context, the sociality of plants in the wild can tell us a lot about the nature of their cultivation and gives us clues how to integrate them into the garden.

A series of different plant populations that coexist within the same habitat form a guild or a plant community. Multiple plant communities become a local ecosystem, varying to some degree over a spatially complex area. You can observe this on a stroll through your favorite park. Perhaps there's a woodland stream that gives way to an open meadow before a change in topography reveals a windy, exposed hillside. In these different communities, different resources such as water and exposure define the palette. While there may be a few common plants to all three, each will likely have a discreet assemblage of plants best adapted to those unique conditions. In between these, you might find gradients ranging from monocultures of a single, highly competitive species or a complex polyculture of many species occupying highly defined niches. Add up all the parks or trails in your region and suddenly you have a local flora with hundreds of species or more that define a visual essence to the landscape. Using this array of wild plant communities as the basis for planting schemes forms one of the essential planks of New Naturalism.

The nature of plants by association is the starting line, not the finish line. These examples are full of variation, which is the key to vibrant landscapes in time and space. They differ in composition, structure, and phenology. But how do all these plants coexist without explosive consequences? Further, if these are templates from which to model planting schemes, how useful are they if they constantly change?

Let's tackle some basic ideas about coexistence first. In wild plant communities, the features and functions of plants act cumulatively and complementarily. Individual species occupy niches because they've evolved to exploit different aspects of the community to minimize the competitive effects between their neighbors. A diverse community of plants can exploit more resources and produce more biomass than a single species could while also forming an integral weft that makes them more resilient over time. Plants exploit these niche opportunities through the array of functional features already discussed, including but not limited to root mass, aboveground architecture, time of flowering, the ability to fix nitrogen, and life history. Cumulatively, the sum of these features is as important as the number of different kinds of plants. With a diverse cohort exhibiting a diversity of traits and sometimes even creating microclimates for themselves, multiple species can coexist at relatively high densities. Higher resident diversity also keeps the tribe together, reducing the likelihood of foreign invasion by using all the resources for those already part of the community.

Change is the underlying engine for how wilderness operates, whether we like it or not. Succession is an ecological principle that accounts for the process of change in the structure of a community (as in which plants succeed others over time). This is different than the kind of short-term, seasonal changes such as precocious floral displays that often occur in response to

(LEFT) Two highly competitive plants—*Artemisia ludoviciana* (Louisiana sage) and *Monarda fistulosa* (wild bergamot)— occupy tight quarters in a tallgrass prairie. Are they duking it out for bragging rights for who can keep this spot the longest? Or is this simply a long-running biological tussle kept in check by other ecological forces?

(BOTTOM) Plants are social creatures, growing densely and competitively where resources permit, as in this shortgrass meadow.

From a gardener's view, the nearly three-foot-tall (1-meter-tall) *I. setosa*, native to wet meadows in Japan, has a totally different habit, phenology, and character than the much-shorter 12-inch-tall (30-cm-tall) forms found in glacial washouts or rocky beaches throughout Canada and the Arctic Circle.

*Packera cana* (woolly groundsel) superficially resembles its distant cousin *Senecio abrotanifolius* (orange-flowered groundsel) in form and function, despite existing on opposite sides of the world. Both are stress-tolerant perennials with a penchant for growing in crevices or on rocky hillsides.

temperature, rainfall, or other environmental variables. Succession shows that there's never an endpoint for a plant community, but rather, a constant forward motion that incorporates disturbance as it happens instead of resisting it. Even if you were to compose a planting of only long-lived species with the desire of having the most permanent planting scheme possible, the time to establish them as a thriving cohort without the incursion of short-lived weeds would likely change your goals within a few seasons. In nature, introduction and recruitment of species is an ongoing process anyway, sort of like gardening.

### The origins of wild and cultivated plants can shed insights into how and where they will grow

Leaving the granular richness of local plant communities behind, it's helpful to take a macro-scale view of ecoregions to understand the broad geographic areas that wild plants call home. An ecoregion is a geographic

collection of various environmental systems that have in common geologic history, topography, soils, and climate. For all of horticultural history's fascination with rare plants from far-flung places, plants with broad distributions are eminently more interesting. What's not to love about a plant that's managed to adapt to a litany of climatic variables and soil across one or more continents? Take *Iris setosa* (beachhead iris), known for its circumpolar distribution from Alaska, Maine, Canada (including the Yukon Territory), Russia, China, Korea, and northern Japan. Across this vast geography, local environments have no doubt influenced millions of plants of *Iris setosa*, perhaps not enough to qualify them as different species, but enough to note when we're thinking about planting them in gardens.

Taken only through the botanical lens, present-day climate is often barely a delineator of plant adaptability or performance in gardens. Across the globe, similar climatic regions often feature interchangeable plant

Around the world, glades and similar communities formed around rock outcrops with minimal soil profiles inspire a New Age approach to making landscapes amid the concrete formations of the built environment. We can use these wild plant palettes to form novel, resilient plantings in cities.

I find as much inspiration for making gardens from roadside wildflowers as I do in the most heralded designed landscapes. These gritty circumstances teem with plants and reveal so much about the value of stress in promoting and managing diversity in gardens.

palettes or even interrelated lineages of plants as evolution has led to sister species essentially performing similar ecological functions in disparate geographies. However, taken in an ecological context, a plant's performance suddenly requires some level of transaction with the ecosystem in which it grows: what other creatures eat it or use it as part of their life cycle? What effect does the plant have on others around it, either chemically, physically, or physiologically? The rationales for a lot of heavyweight horticultural selections become short-winded on this account, which isn't disqualifying, but certainly not worth a merit award. Nothing is static, biologically speaking, but some plants are more active than others in this way. Nativity often means a plant has a greater capacity to transact within the ecological economy as I'll describe in the following section. If we're to hasten the biological average around the globe, our gardens, however globally inspired, should do with a little more local color.

Gardens planted in strict adherence to these biogeographic ideas might feature predominantly native plants. That leads into some controversial territory when attempting to define what is native. Without launching into pages of semantics, the best mechanism for solving the native versus nonnative dilemma might be a quote from the Greek philosopher Heraclitus: "the only constant in nature is change itself." Native is defined for this book as a plant that's indigenous to a given place within the last 12,000 years, a unit of time proposed by some scientists as the maximum amount of time an ecosystem can go unchanged before some variation, disruption, or transition. Despite their terrestrial nature, plants disperse by seeds and other vegetative structures, moving much more slowly absent the agility of two or four legs. But this dispersal can allow plants to migrate over tens of thousands of years into new habitats more suitable to their optimal growth. Global climate change will scramble all

of this, admittedly, with the consequence of extinction for some species that will just run out of time to adapt or migrate to new habitats. In attempting to strengthen connectivity across the greater landscape, utilizing native plants from wild places in gardens can strengthen gene flow, create additional populations and reservoirs of genetic diversity, and support the development of more habitats for the organisms that

This garden-discovered aster named 'Lalla' likely owes its lineage to *Symphyotrichum novae-angliae* and *S. oblongifolium*, a horticultural happy accident that's both beautiful and ecologically valuable. It is often one of the last asters to flower in the growing season, ensuring floral resources remain available for invertebrates late into the season.

rely on them for their existence. Think of planting as a series of steppingstones that connect populations across the landscape.

Leading with natives on the structural scale of the landscape doesn't preclude plant diversity on a finer scale. The term "near native" refers to plants not historically native to your area but which occur within the same general region or hemisphere. The near native definition also extends to related species often within the same genus with similar growth and flowering habits, even if they aren't from the same geographic location. If we return to the wild for a moment, it's clear that a single plant species' contemporary wild distribution doesn't tell the whole story of its evolutionary lineage. Humans are canny dispersers. Research increasingly shows that native peoples around the world, predating modern colonialization of dominant ethnic and cultural groups, had deep, abiding relationships with the land. Their wildside gardening some 5,000 to 10,000 years prior to modern civilization certainly had a lasting effect on the landscapes we know and grow today. Dispersal comes with consequences, some positive and others negative. The real tale of how and why plants occur where they do is deeper and more complex and quickly denudes arguments of nativity, especially given the present era of climate change. A distribution is informed by a plant's ability to disperse, establish, and thrive where it lands. Plants don't play by our rules; they predate human evolution by hundreds of millions of years and often have more elastic natural profiles than we give them credit for. Whatever observations we can make now are merely convenient insights into relatively recent history.

Then, of course, there's the subject of plants that have passed through the hands of humanity, derived from horticultural activities. A cultivar is a portmanteau formed from the combination of the words "cultivated and variety," which, for all its intended simplicity, creates a lot of confusion among otherwise literate people. The International Code of Nomenclature for Cultivated Plants (2009) defines a cultivar as:

> an assemblage of plants that (a) has been selected for a particular character or combination of characters, (b) is distinct, uniform and stable in those characters, and (c) when propagated by appropriate means, retains those characters.

In this definition, cultivars are plants grown in landscapes that have intentionally resulted from some selection effort and can be propagated without losing the value of that selection, whether that's ornamental, physiological, or otherwise. Where arguments usually start is at the intersection of how cultivars are developed or propagated and for what traits. Indeed, many cultivars represent genetic aberrations (such as doubles or unusual color breaks), exceptions that natural

processes produce but which might quickly be surpassed in fitness by other phenotypes. Many cultivars of a distinctive, singular phenotype are propagated asexually via tissue culture or other vegetative methods—cloning plants, essentially. Cultivars can also be selected for disease resistance, the ability to perform in particular conditions, or general horticultural qualities such as longer bloom seasons, denser growth habits, or a hundred other reasons. The motivation for selecting and developing a cultivar might have roots in novelty and variation, but the result and all its merits (or demerits) are otherwise hard to categorize.

Fundamentally, there is no conclusion that can be made whether cultivars have or do not have ecological value. Ecologically speaking, not all cultivars are created equal and not all cultivars are created. The definition of a cultivar doesn't permit such generalizations without more probing questions. As such, there's no need to hastily condemn plants selected for horticultural applications simply because they carry a name bearing evidence of some intention. Instead, we have to know something about the cultivar (whether it's clonal or derived from seed) and how it persists (is it sterile, asexually propagated, or can it exchange genes with other plants of the same species even if the progeny aren't identical to the parents) in order to judge whether it will be resilient and have ecological merit. Emerging research has illustrated that any assessment of a cultivar's ecological merits depends on the characters being investigated, whether flower or leaf color, changes to a flower's structure, or modifications of a plant's overall growth habit. In these studies, some cultivars do very little in terms of providing ecosystem services to pollinators or other wildlife and may not thrive on their own without some form of gardening life support of human intervention to maintain or control growth through fertility, water, or mechanical means. Other cultivars actually outperform generic examples of the species when measured for their ability to attract and sustain pollinators or to grow and perform under garden conditions. In the best-case scenarios, cultivars represent highly fit phenotypes, genetic fingerprints that might be the linchpin for success in otherwise difficult environments (such as an urban center) that has few precedents to wild natural history. This linchpin is all the more valuable when these cultivars either persist for a long period (and thus perform ecological services year after year) or can exchange genes with other plants, produce populations that might vary from the original phenotype over time, and still maintain a sufficient level of landscape performance. We don't always welcome phenotypic change—if you bought a variety with purple flowers for its purple flowers, you might be disappointed when plants start to arise that have white flowers. Yet some find this enchanting and curious, a petri dish experiment of genetics.

In the end, your decision whether to use cultivars should be based on how it grows, reproduces, and contributes to the landscape's ecological trajectory. Plants that thrive and support other forms of life should always find a place in gardens because they form the critical components of lively, thriving vegetation. Five gardeners in your neighborhood with wilder, more diverse, eco-centric gardens far outweigh one of them growing a few double-flowered varieties with silly names.

### Plants have coevolved with other organisms to form dynamic webs of life

Even if your principle interest in making a wilder garden is your fascination with plants, you can't help but enjoy and explore the lives of their cohorts. In so many ways, the features that add to the richness of life in your garden are often things you already have but simply haven't activated, such as a dead stump or small basin for water. Open and preferably moving water is critical for almost all animals. Even a small amount can attract dragonflies, amphibians, birds, and bats, which also put pressure on populations of mosquitos, fungus gnats, and flies. Still water provides habitat for pests such as mosquitoes but utilizing submersible tablets containing the beneficial bacteria *Bacillus thuringiensis* will keep them at bay without adversely affecting other creatures.

While plants might serve as foundational producers of ecosystems around the world in conjunction with the soil biome, they obviously don't exist in a vacuum. The botanical insights throughout this chapter often have an animal dimension. The floral resources and seeds of legumes, which you might have selected for their nitrogen-fixing ability, factor heavily into the diets of birds, insects, and small mammals. Tall, architectural perennials such as *Silphium* (cup plants), *Eupatorium*, and *Eutrochium* (Joe-pye weeds) often feature hollow stems, which form veritable insect condos for nesting and overwintering. They do double duty by creating structure for plantings. Interestingly, late-blooming, long-lived perennials in the aster family have been shown in research studies to serve as insectaries for beneficial insects, which are natural enemies. Other plant families have examples of this, but the aster family seems to lead in stride. The natural world's equivalent of frenemies, including natural predators such as mantids, spiders, beetles, lacewings, and dragonflies, helps strike a balance with herbivores in the garden ecosystem.

The fact that flowering plants attract more than pollinating insects is a good thing, even if it challenges gardeners to accept that something will eat their beloved plants, also known as herbivory. This initial aversion to the cosmetic damage of plants stems from a nurturing ornamental tradition that prizes blue-ribbon specimens that reflect on a gardener's ability to cultivate them. But think of it this way: if nothing is eating your plants, what life is your garden really supporting? When you grow populations of plants, what does it matter if a small percentage of leaves support a host of other creatures? With herbivory there are tradeoffs between what is browsed and what regrows. Some plants regrow, sprouting new shoots from stems or crowns and continue unabated. Other plants with more conservative growth habits can be all but eliminated from the planting. Feeding choices for generalist browsers such as deer and other mammals are relative to the abundance and availability of the food supply and the overall size of the browsing population. Insects tend to eat a more limited range of plants, even if generalist species can host on a broader range of plants than specialists. Tiny holes in leaves pale in comparison to

(TOP) In smaller gardens where a water garden or larger water feature might not be feasible, a simple source of water can become a keystone for life within lush, diverse plantings.

(LEFT) Increasingly, science recognizes the ecological value of densely planted gardens as small patches of habitats for an array of creatures including pollinators, birds, reptiles, amphibians, and small mammals.

the total decimation of plant populations by mammalian herbivores. Many studies have shown that for all the eating that can happen in our gardens, herbivores tend to consume no more than 20 percent of total net primary production in a growing season. Considering all the leaves, stems, flowers, and fruits produced by all plants in a growing season, that's not such a bad tradeoff for pollination services and an ecologically intact food web right in your own backyard. All of this underscores the principle values of diverse planting schemes. With more plants in gardens, the effects of any one creature largely go unnoticed. Similarly, when we grow gardens with healthy microbial communities absent juicy, nutrient-rich fertilizers that favor only the most voracious biomass accumulators, we create gardens with less succulent, less palatable foliage for herbivores. Nature doesn't play favorites; everything ultimately gets eaten by something else or returns to the soil through the web of life.

While plants and their communities are the focus of this book, you can endeavor to provide a richness of habitats for the pollinators, natural predators, birds, mammals, amphibians, and reptiles that stand a chance of frequenting your garden on account of increased plant diversity. As this chapter demonstrates, ecology isn't a switch to flip—the lamp is already on.

## 2   UNDERSTANDING PLACES FOR PLANTING

**MY LIFELONG ROMANCE** for making gardens swings like a hammock between two trees—one firmly rooted in curation, the act of studying, collecting, and organizing plants, and one in creation, the process of planting for a new beginning. Subtending my interest in curation is a passion for matching a palette of plants with the potential of place. Understanding place is the next leg of the ecological gardening adventure, embracing landscapes for their soils, topography, climate, and vegetation instead of erasing them in search of a blank canvas. Admittedly, a blank canvas provides an easier starting place and sometimes is truly the best way to begin in order to undo a recent history of land use that leaves more scars than fond memories. In urban

landscapes engineered to the nth degree, you may not have any choice to begin with. It's for this reason that planting with a sense of place matters now more than ever, as if to extend an invitation to the natural world as it may have hopes of deriving a precedent for what it could be again. As both a noun and verb, planting is simultaneously a result and a brave act: to plant is to have hope in what a planting might become.

At the outset of a new planting, you should cultivate wild hopes that the result might yield in excess of your greatest expectations while being wide-eyed with reality: you and I are not magicians. The best we can do is empower our gardening with the botanical and ecological insights from chapter 1—the rules of engagement. But the match needs a court, so we turn now to the site. At this intersection between plants, gardeners, and the nature of place, gardens can be more than a collection of planted things that we've willed into existence. Sites are vessels for plantings; plantings are content for sites.

Certain charismatic plants evoke a sense of place by virtue of their colors, characters, and phenology, such as this late-season duo of *Vernonia altissima* (giant ironweed) and *Sorghastrum nutans* (Indiangrass).

## GROUND RULES FOR MAKING GARDENS: THE NOT-SO-BIG PICTURE

In many ways, the picture about making gardens isn't that big at all: most gardens are small. The kind of expansive, public-scale planting schemes that have inspired a contemporary renaissance in naturalistic horticulture require some reprogramming in order to work for the home garden, even though they offer ample inspiration. In the United States, the median size of a residential lot is 0.20 acres (810 m²) and in highly urbanized areas, it's considerably less. In smaller gardens, even those under one-half acre, the scales for experiencing planting become intimate and even more ingredient-centric. Paradoxically, it's in these settings where the fleeting nature of plants, however enjoyable in close proximity, requires exaggeration. With less space to create complex schemes and patterns of scale, every feature of plants has the potential to contribute mightily to the visual and ecological result.

Even in a small garden ecology happens. Nature isn't confined to major outposts as our conservation parks and preserves, for all their necessity and worth, would have us believe. Nature is flitting around us daily, if only we'd notice or give it a space to thrive in earnest. The size of your yard matters little to the foraging butterfly that finds nectar from flowers there or the field mouse milling around for seeds and the neighborhood hawk watching its every move. While the size of your yard might have something to do with how these organisms inhabit it, it doesn't preclude the opportunity for cultivating habitat while you make a beautiful garden. A garden based on dynamic communities of plants can serve as a backdrop to social functions and outdoor entertaining while also harboring biodiversity, if even as a refuge from the clamor of urbanity. Your green patch in tandem with the others in your neighborhood cumulatively forms a macro-scale landscape, a weft of smaller places held together with threads of environmental form. It might seem improbable that your home garden could rise to the standard of such ecological goodness, but the world is full of examples in research and practice that suggest otherwise. Put together, the space occupied by residential neighborhoods far outpaces that held in public parks or preserves. Our gardens, however small, can be up to something good with the potential to ecologically rethread the world.

### Find Inspiration Everywhere but Stay Grounded

It's easy to field inspirations from Instagram and Pinterest, but gardening isn't like painting a wall. The materials aren't inert, and the process takes longer, often with multiple and ever-changing results. Flower show gardens, like this one shown from Hampton Court Flower Show (p. 37), don't represent horticultural reality, but they do capture the dream of a freer, wilder kind of gardening, even if impressionistically. How do you reconcile the dream garden with the one you have outside the kitchen window? You can't forget the emotional and romantic ambition for making gardens alongside the too-often-ignored principles of making them functional and successful. You have to be honest about where to start the gardening adventure and accept that reality not out of austerity, but, as a precursor to success. Be aware of your site in all its many dimensions.

Your first inspiration might be growing in front of you. You can start by choosing plants with the ability to do something more than just look pretty. Traditionally, plants form the basis for how we define spaces in the garden or satisfy criteria for the kind of landscape we want. But even if you're planting a windbreak or a tree for shade, you can make a dynamic choice that satisfies ornamental and ecological needs. Why not substitute for a plant that checks many boxes, such as attractive flowers, handsome fall colors, and abundant fruits for birds, rather than something that only checks one of those? If you're looking for "groundcover," why not opt for "green mulch"—a dense, diverse layer of plantings close to the ground—to reduce unwanted weeds and create richer garden habitats? This doesn't have to be rote filler, and in some ways, it's the best excuse for planting more plants.

(TOP LEFT) Dreamy planting schemes such as this one at the RHS's Hampton Court Flower Show (UK) inspire our imagination with romantic notions, often beyond the realm of possibility. But in doing so, we learn to appreciate the beauty of ephemerality and how a diverse palette makes for complex, captivating vignettes.

(TOP RIGHT) The unending, immersive feeling of a grassland inspires complicated feelings for some people—for some elation, for others discomfort—even though some form of it covers nearly 40 percent of the planet. Most parts of the world have some precedent for it in managed landscapes, but at home, consider the scale at which you garden and how you can plant proactively to achieve a sense of place.

(BOTTOM LEFT) American composer Aaron Copland often said that every note counts; the same can be said of plant choices. This residential planting along a driveway in a midcentury planned development is about 2,000 square feet (186 square meters) but contains 46 different kinds of plants, over 60 percent of which are native to the region or derived from native species. This photo was taken approximately one year after planting.

## EVALUATING SITES TO ACHIEVE A SENSE OF PLACE

Rarely does a lush, diverse garden spring from bare soil without some understanding of place. Often our garden journeys begin by way of inheritance—a gangly hedge alongside an old house, the remnants of a former gardener's attempts to make use of the land, or ill-conceived plantings dotted into the lawn with good intentions and hellish results. Regardless of whether you're remodeling or starting from scratch, there is a palette for every garden and every gardener, a working assemblage that marries features of and fascinations with plants to the form of the site. While a sense of place doesn't have to rule with tyranny over every landscaping decision you make, respecting and cultivating it can reveal a deeper, more satisfying, and honest experience with a garden full of individuality and authenticity.

Marcia and Randy Tatroe's garden in suburban Denver, CO, USA, celebrates high and dry gardening with a signature collection of regionally adapted plants such as *Agave havardiana* (Harvard's century plant) joined by tulips and grape hyacinths that reseed in their climate.

Several hundred *Camassia leichtlinii* 'Caerulea' (great blue camas) in my Long Look Prairie color the spine of the planting in mid-spring, thriving on surface runoff in heavy clay soil. While not native to my immediate context, they are well situated in context with the site.

### Start small with durable assumptions

If you're so inspired to reconceive your entire approach to gardening, remember the buffet line lesson—it's easy for your eyes to be bigger than your plate. Regardless of how much space you garden in or what you have to start with, begin your adventure in New Naturalism at a manageable scale so that you can explore and experiment. Smallness doesn't limit the possibilities or undermine the purpose; it's realistic. A garden is a place of pleasure, creativity, and some expectation of work. Keeping things right-sized to the demands of a busy lifestyle just makes sense, unless you want to be indentured to your garden every growing season.

Traditional ornamental gardens often require more work because of the way we've created them. They have existed purely based on what they look like instead of what they might do. Sometimes these artful gardens have existed in spite of us: it's easy to keep a planting looking sharp, provided you have enough time and money. Conversely, it's also fairly easy to create a garden where the inherent tendencies of plants run the show, provided you (or your neighbors) don't care what anything looks like. While you might get lucky every now and again, the chances of arriving at the perfect balance of beauty and ecology without intention are fairly low.

Making durable assumptions at the outset and throughout the gardening process keeps your approach grounded to place. A durable assumption is more than a best guess—it's educated and calculated, if not foolproof. With durable assumptions you won't always be right, but with any luck you won't always be wrong. Your goal should be less about winning or losing, but, most importantly, about staying in the game. Durable assumptions are inherently site-specific—it's much easier to embrace the nature of place than to be on a constant quest to alter it. The further you deviate from the site as you find it, the more resources it will require both to establish and manage it. I know many gardeners who coddle water-hogging plants in otherwise dry soils with regular watering. There's nothing resilient about an act of devotion to the plants you love; there is more to gardening than this. Durable assumptions should help you feel confident in the results. Be realistic about what plants will grow appropriately without life support. This is no moment for zonal denial; rather, it's time for curating a palette that will thrive, not merely survive. The plants that thrive will become the mainstays of the garden, the foundation of your garden's style and success.

### To land on a good plan, observe your site and ask questions

While I can't prescribe a list of seminal, durable assumptions for each situation you might encounter, I can encourage you to ask questions. To know something about the place you intend to plant requires a process of enquiry, which isn't a task you accomplish on one sunny Sunday afternoon in May. It's a process that continues for the life of the garden. What does this site tell you that can inform making a garden that belongs there versus one inscribed upon the land? Planting and gardening should harmonize with the nature of the site, an understanding gained from observation, experimentation, and recursive learning. These are slow processes compared to those employed by two shovel-ready landscapers with a truck. Gardeners should be good students of place and work to evaluate and guide the structure of the landscape, its function, and how it will change.

The standard regimen of site analysis involves assessment of the status quo with an assumption that a gardener will quickly get to work remaking the site. What if, instead, the analysis of a site's climate, context, topography, soil, and exposure became a guide for what's possible, instead of an initial condition that needs alteration? Accounting for real challenges and opportunities is perhaps the most important part of analyzing sites. Regardless of the perceived challenges of any site, there are often more opportunities hidden one layer beneath the surface.

Evaluating place begins with climate. At least two-thirds of the success of plants in place is due to this interrelated phenomenon of annual temperature and precipitation patterns. In the current Anthropocene epoch, when climate rules are rapidly changing, you

should be open-eyed and honest about these effects on the landscape. Understand how much and when precipitation falls. Check your hardiness zone and understand your annual winter minimum temperature, even if it's merely one part of the larger picture. My annual winter minimum temperature is around -15 degrees Fahrenheit (-26 degrees Celsius), but in the last 10 years it has varied from -22 degrees (-30 degrees Celsius) to just 0 degrees Fahrenheit (-17.7 degrees Celsius). This kind of variance is maddening for plants and gardeners, but it foretells a stark reality of the future. Many climate change models for the Northern Hemisphere predict a 5- to 7-degree latitudinal shift toward the equator, meaning climate today is going to look quite different by the end of the century. For that, so will your garden. For some parts of the world this will mean more frequent droughts, and for others it will mean seasonal inundations without historic precedent. Some places might experience both extremes in a single year. Generalist plant species that run the planet likely have the plasticity to withstand these changes but using them in landscapes may require different and more durable assumptions. Species with more finite, specific requirements will likely be challenged to persist and thrive both in wild and man-made places.

To fit a climate-specific garden to place, it's important to acknowledge the immediate context in which your landscape resides so you can embrace place and not prepare to battle it. Most gardeners underestimate the potential of landscapes at the outset as if Mother Nature were outmatching our every move. In the spirit of asking good questions, consider where you are: continental or coastal? Urban or country? What is the history of the land's use by humans? What vegetation, native or otherwise, already exists on the site and how does it influence the land? You'll have to frame these questions both in past and present terms. For example, the enclosed canopies of woodlands won't spring up overnight in the middle of a windy, open field simply because you want them to. Conversely, trying to create a meadow in the middle of the woods will require nearly constant interventions with tree seedlings and suckers keen on colonizing the space. Be realistic and process

The mature canopy of *Quercus alba* (white oaks) gives this garden a uniquely regional frame to fill with an abundant herbaceous picture, dominated in late summer by the short-lived *Rudbeckia triloba* (brown-eyed Susan). By acknowledging and embracing the canopy as an opportunity of place, the garden teems with local biodiversity and inspires weekend adventurers to seek out life within it.

*Stipa gigantea* (giant needlegrass) translates light throughout the day into an aesthetic feature while serving as a structural matrix in this planting at the Royal Horticultural Society Garden Wisley.

oriented. Recognize and take note of existing natural features, vegetation, and microclimates, from ditches to dead trees. These opportunities often reveal the authentic character of place or give clues to how it might have been influenced by human activity in recent history, even if ultimately you have to fill in the ditch or cut down the dead tree. But embracing these features can be practical. The presence of a ditch or swale might give you a clue about how water moves across the site, perhaps one of the most important topographic observations you can make. Topographic themes such as hills, valleys, swales, and subtle changes in slope all present different canvasses for applying and presenting plant communities, as well as different microclimates for establishing them. In my own Long Look Prairie, the core of the planting—tall, architectural grasses including cultivars of *Panicum virgatum* (switchgrass) and *Andropogon gerardii* (big bluestem)—follows the line of water with a tall matrix of grasses and sedges that mitigate seasonal surface runoff. This X-shaped array

forms a legible spine from which the rest of the planting grows. While you may desire to remove existing vegetation, it can give clues to what has thrived successfully on the site prior to you. If it's well situated and of value, you might decide to keep or even amplify it, whether it's native or not. If it's a large tree, removing it isn't without consequence. In a shaded woodland, the loss of canopy opens the understory to disturbance, which as a gardener you may view as an opportunity or a detriment.

It's worth taking an inventory of the visual themes of the site, which can enhance your landscape's authenticity and sense of place. These might come both from natural and architectural borrowed views such as distant mountains or even the facade of a nearby building. While some views are desirable, you may want to screen others or at least distract from them, all of which plants can accomplish (and more cost effectively than hardscapes or construction). In the same way, consider the lines you have to work with both on-site and nearby. Storied landscape architects such as Frederick Law Olmsted eschewed straight lines, preferring to fabricate a feeling of nature through the use of curves and soft angles when laying out beds, walkways, and groupings of plants. After all, there's surely no organism in the history of the planet that's as fascinated by straight lines as humans. Yet such linearity abounded in 19th-century European gardens, reflecting the architectural styles of everything from country homes and farm buildings to row houses and city mansions, even as planting styles loosened and found more natural inspirations. Your own style might eventually intervene but start with place as you get to know the land on which you garden.

Certain plants in your local flora might form the gestalt of your landscape; they sort of just look like they belong. Historic neighborhoods in urban areas often feature monoculture tree canopies, representing one or a few popular (or perhaps enduring) choices made centuries ago. In many cities, contemporary urban forestry has rightfully sought to diversify these canopies but may not have exerted an influence on the look or character of the landscape yet. My neighborhood is called Oak Park, an obvious reference to natural (and planted) stands of several different species of oaks that line the streets and viewsheds throughout the area. If I were to lose a tree in my garden to storm damage, you can bet I'll plant an oak to keep with local terroir.

The type of soil you have, its texture, and productivity should inform almost all of your planting decisions—you have to dig down before you can grow up. Soil is alive with microorganisms, not merely an inert medium in which plants root. It's almost always an opportunity. A soil test can often give you the physical and chemical properties of the soil, but may come packaged in recommendations that make no sense for a resilient garden. It's so easy to fall into the trap of role playing a farmer at home, feeling that the soil needs accessorizing or augmenting in order to produce something. It's true that in and around new construction, native soils become heavily compacted, riddled with debris, or removed entirely and replaced with infill from anywhere. In these degraded and disturbed circumstances, augmenting the planting layer with sand or screened compost may be necessary to establish plants that can get to work making soil over time. In more established residential conditions, soils often have plenty of mineral and nutritional capacity to support a broad planting palette. We just have to fit the palette to place: the resources available (or unavailable) in the soil will favor some plants over others.

Light is the final consideration for creating space and situating plants, the architectures of which can give you clues for where they have naturally evolved. Larger leaves tend to abound in shaded circumstances where more surface area captures more light. Smaller leaves and conservative growth are favored in stressful conditions where an economical approach guarantees a longer lifespan. Many plants have the plasticity to respond to subtle changes in exposure, often occurring over a range of conditions in wild circumstances. Plants native to transitional edge communities have the most plasticity because they've evolved under conditions subject to seasonal and long-term changes as competition favors the proliferation of different plants in time and space. Plants of grasslands and woodland edges often look different across this gradient of exposure, growing more densely in sun and more conservatively in shade.

Finally, don't forget to notice how light changes across the site even in a single day. Practically speaking, it matters to know how many hours of sun or shade a particular area of the landscape receives. But plant shapes and architectures translate light in ways that add intimacy, mystery, and intrigue to the landscape experience. If you ever have lain on your back and stared at the sky through the canopy of a tree, you'll understand just how magical and calming that experience can be as your eyes balance the contrast between light and shadow. East Asian garden traditions are full of inspirational examples of plants used or placed strictly for their shapely interplay with light. Some plants such as *Deschampsia cespitosa* (tufted hair grass) or *Stipa gigantea* (giant needle grass) read so well with side- or backlighting that not to situate them accordingly misses out on the breadth of their personality and interest.

Site analysis can shed insights into the habits of other creatures in your garden, which should influence the shape of your planting areas. Scientific literature has long established the relationship between the size of a habitat and how it functions, although often this discussion is in the context of planning for parks or nature preserves. The axiom: smaller patches with a greater surface to interior area ratio are more prone to disturbance and reduce the amount of core habitat available. Bed edges are ecologically porous and receive disturbance from the landscape around them. Of course, the nature of the human-dominated landscape is already quite patchy, so at first blush, this seems moot. Avoiding patchiness in the home garden may not even be feasible, but we could infer that placing paths toward the margins of plantings (versus one that might run right through it) helps preserve as much core space from disturbance as possible. This increased interior area can result in denser, lusher plantings with fewer gaps for weeds, a sort of self-sustaining microclimate created by the planting. In theory, perfect circles and squares, which have greater interior areas relative to surface area, are the geometrically ideal planting bed shapes from an ecological perspective. The bottom line—even as you adopt a practical approach to New Naturalism—is to keep in mind that the size and shape of an ecological garden is as important for how it looks and grows as it is to the wildlife that you endeavor to attract.

Of course, all of this is somewhat relative to the nature of the landscape beyond your garden. Are you close to a large woodland or open area? Does your garden grow near a waterway? All these opportunities for wildlife movement in your neighborhood increase the value of your planting as a square (or circle) in the green patchwork of your local ecosystem. Movement is different for different creatures too. The wider and more generous the corridors of similar vegetation, the more wildlife benefits you can expect. If your landscape is near a woodland, this could translate into planting similar tree canopy species as those in adjoining areas. By relating canopies to one another, you create a continuous corridor of vegetation through which wildlife can move, nestling your plantings into the greater context of the landscape. Migratory birds often look for these vegetation corridors when scanning for places to rest and forage. If you have an existing canopy, you might consider how to enrich its understory to support small mammals and reptiles as they move through the property. I happened to get lucky by establishing a path between my prairie and hedgerow that coincidentally aligns with the local deer population's route. I'm not exactly fond of the browsing they do along the way, but there's little point fighting it. I gird the edges of the path at key points with shrubs such as *Salix purpurea* (purple osier willow), *Spiraea alba* (meadowsweet), and *Acer negundo* (box elder) that they are less prone to browse in hopes of steering them to the exit.

An increase in the structural diversity of plants will increase species diversity, particularly birds and insects. This means more than just a few nice trees and a patch of perennials. It encourages us to think about planting a diverse canopy of small and large trees, utilizing shrubs underneath, and plant richly in the herbaceous layers. This principle supports the trend throughout the world that woodlands tend to contain more species than grasslands—the richness of habitats creates niches for an abundance of species. In one study of woodland ecosystems, a developed canopy layer was responsible for the addition of 3 to 15 times as many animal species compared to shrub and ground-cover layers, respectively. The creatures we share the garden with value complex places.

### After a study of place, define spaces for living and moving

Of course, gardens aren't just places for plants to grow—they are places for life in its many forms. How you intend to use your landscape will play some role in determining the character and composition of plant communities. Creating a garden that thrives while supporting a modern lifestyle begins by asking yourself how you intend to live with the garden. Do you need to consider play spaces for children, a vegetable garden, or flexible space for future building projects? How you intend to move through the garden or experience it once planted will determine where paths should go

or how they flow. Considering how you intend to walk the dog or take a morning stroll with cup of coffee can reveal a lot about where plantings might make sense in relationship to you and the rest of the property. Sometimes movement alone can define garden spaces more powerfully than any other form of space usage and can predict how ecologically vibrant these spaces can be for wildlife.

Begin crafting a plan by considering how these spaces relate to existing plantings, if any, and the other features you took inventory of earlier. You can do this on paper or by gesticulating to your spouse or a friend. I collect the fallen sticks from a row of decades-old *Celtis occidentalis* (hackberries) to mark paths in my garden and outline new projects as I wander around dreaming. As the season goes on, they slowly break down and fade into the vegetation, but in the moment, my curious little stick arrangements constitute an inexpensive,

therapeutic method for defining space. You could use whatever your site gives you, boulders to bricks. Just choose something temporary that gives you creative license to explore the makings of an accommodating, plant-driven garden.

This real-time accounting of what you can so easily observe forms a framework for gardens as opposed to random acts of planting (from which many of us have learned the hard lesson that small trees can grow far larger than we ever thought they would). Existing masses, either built or planted, can become skeletons for

---

A good plan, even a conceptual one in your head, is only as good as its execution. Naturalistic plantings can boast the most biodiversity in the neighborhood but fail to win over any of your neighbors (or spouse) if they can't visually make sense of what you're up to.

The laterally trained, pendulous branches of *Cedrus atlantica* 'Glauca Pendula' (weeping Atlas cedar) at Wave Hill's Wild Garden in the Bronx, New York, anchors the horizon line. It provides a strong backdrop to the softer, complex, and detailed vignettes with vertical echoes from *Verbascum* (mullein) hybrids and *Foeniculum vulgare* (fennel).

planting schemes. Imagine interplanting a taller woody hedgerow with shrubs, herbaceous groundcovers, and perennials or extending the garden underneath the canopy for a woodland experience (see chapter 6). Open spaces tend to invite more herbaceous-dominated planting schemes with perhaps the occasional intercession of a shrub or small tree (see chapter 4). The edges between these spaces become opportunities, in some cases harboring more niches for unique plantings, portals, and passageways through plantings for the greatest experience (see chapter 6). Gardens created using this method become more immersive and authentic, less contrived than simply imagining scenes with plants employed as paint and sculpture. The goal isn't to confine plants within bed lines to look at as a portrait on a wall, but to create plant-driven places at home, engines for life and living.

### Use legible frames to visually organize your wilder garden

The anatomy of a garden, the legible framework within which you grow and experience plants, is the most accessible place to start organizing garden spaces. Orderly, legible frames help make sense of our efforts by communicating intention (instead of a garden looking, to some, like a runaway train). The pathways defined by a census of movement through your property are the first steps toward legibly framing planting areas. If you prefer a curvilinear approach, these sinuous and meandering edges shape the spaces for naturalistic plantings and frame them to the viewer. Hard, straight edges—such as the concrete lines replete in the built environment—can communicate culturally recognizable forms of care and intention. Inside these grounded frames, you can explore space with plants as you might a collection of favorite things in a living room. The architecture of your home or surrounding buildings might further influence your approach to lines and frames. This is a highly subjective realm of which a majority opinion of good taste tends to prevail with regard to which types of lines work with home or property styles. I am usually more concerned with content of the spaces, although in the chapters dedicated to planting palettes, I'll offer suggestions where appropriate in the best interest of the plantings. Keep in mind for all the architectural agonizing one can do on a new site, migratory birds and garden-dwelling amphibians take no notice of well-placed golden angles or rules of thirds.

Nowhere in this book will you encounter a sketched planting plan with dots on a page prescribing the locations of all the plants on your list. Good garden design is less about drawings that represent ideas or static plans, but, rather, more a form of judgement that responds to and considers space, plants, and long-range goals. While well-documented plans have merit for commercial and professional projects, the process of making a home garden should feel less strict without pressures of precision and accuracy. Your home landscape, if ever in a plan view, should have plenty of doodles, scribbles, and strikes as you negotiate the reality of planting with the reality of site.

Perhaps most importantly, never stop asking questions, even as the garden establishes and changes with time. The site-specific approach requires more than just an initial assessment, but, rather, an ongoing one that accounts for the ecology of the garden, including your life within it. This philosophy of practice can help you course correct in the early years when planting choices might falter or fail. In the long view, it gives you a method to engage with the landscape instead of merely applying plants, ideas, and features to it.

Through all of this, it's admirable to modify the site as little as possible, though this isn't always feasible. Tillage and soil disturbance can reverse decades of natural soil-building processes, introduce compaction, and ultimately release more carbon instead of sequestering it. But mitigating grade changes or introducing hardscapes is simply part of how to integrate human lifestyles into landscapes. Throughout construction, new microclimates form within sites that might have previously been more homogeneous. Introducing disturbance to sites isn't exactly unnatural, particularly if it gives rise to new opportunities for plantings—even in nature, disturbance and diversity often go hand in hand.

(TOP) At Great Dixter, the home and garden of the late Christopher Lloyd, paths on axis with the house create a legible frame with which to navigate and understand the ebullient plantings.

(LEFT) The tall evergreen back-drop is essential to reading and enjoying this florally rich planting. Without such a clean, uniform background, the incredible detail might be lost to visual competition from other features, never mind the canny color echo. This represents a classic orderly frame for a beautiful, if not also disorderly, planting.

## MATCH PLANTS TO PLACE

Even after a thoughtful assessment of place, resilient gardens only succeed with resonant plantings. Traditionally, many landscapes are an exception to their surroundings without any relation to the nature of place. While we can dig the hole, it doesn't mean a plant has any fundamental purpose in that place or that it will survive without onerous resources. For many, this act of life support defines gardening. But why not consider life that sustains itself?

Understanding plants in context, specifically your context, can lead you to answer the coalescing question of New Naturalism: what plants would thrive in a garden of this place? Whether you're an avid enthusiast or experienced gardener, you can start to appreciate the palette of plants you know and grow with greater awareness for how they thrive in your garden. Despite all the science to draw from as presented in chapter 1, there's no precise approach for each site that could easily be repeated with the expectation of the same results. The recursive nature of gardening on the wild side requires the discipline to match plants to place.

### Borrowing clues from wild plant habitats can inform how you use them in gardens

Since childhood, I have been fascinated with plants in wild places, even before I really understood them. I marveled at finding delicately flowered lilies such as *Lilium michiganense* (Michigan's lily) and *L. philadelphicum* (wood lily) tucked in along the unkempt edges of woods and thickets as they gave way to open space. I couldn't help but wonder how something so seemingly fragile succeeded against all that encroachment. The interstitial habitat created at this tattered, natural boundary actually suits the former just fine. It thrived in my woodland garden with midday sun and shade throughout the rest of the day. But for *Lilium philadelphicum*, more often a prairie plant, this edge environment almost always foretold the decline of the population over time unless some disturbance thinned or removed the canopy. Shade was its encumbrance. At any rate, *L. philadelphicum* is also less adaptable to

(TOP) Placelessness is abundant in modern architecture and landscape architecture, a trend towards universal blandness at the expense of regional vibrancy. So many gardens could seemingly happen anywhere in total disregard to context. While this show garden planting is full of artistic flair (and safe to critique since it's not a real garden), what more could it do if it were a real planting somewhere? The only way to answer that question is to know where "somewhere else" would be.

(OPPOSITE TOP) The ultimate garden habitat features a layered design that thoughtfully applies plants to place to emulate the structure of wild habitats.

(OPPOSITE BOTTOM LEFT) Species of *Aralia*, a horticulturally and botanically curious genus of mostly large shrubs and small trees native to Asia and the Americas, form mid-level canopies with distinctive fanlike leaves. In their native habitats, because of their colonial tendencies, these charismatic trees can regenerate and respond to stress or environmental changes.

(OPPOSITE BOTTOM RIGHT) *Lilium michiganense* (Michigan's lily).

garden culture for whatever reason, but when it does, it thrives in full sun and soil with good drainage.

These insights about wild plant habitats pepper field guides and floras written by botanists and local experts, but rarely translate into insights that make their way onto gardeners' radars. Despite a dearth of specifics, we know that plants are adapted to place in a variety of ways, principally by their anatomy, physiology, and phenology (as described in chapter 1). Sure, it would be lovely if we could just zip to any part of the globe on a constant botanical vacation in search of insights and experiences with each plant about which we wanted to know more. But with so many floras online, it's convenient to pick up information about the origins of garden plants and where they might occur in the wild. (For cultivars, knowing something about the origins of the parents can shed some light on how to grow them, although sometimes this information can be as confounding as it is helpful.) Plant origins give clues about how they will grow in gardens and interact with other plants acting as a spotlight on the underlying ecology of the region or ecosystem. Even without an ecology degree, you can interpret what you see visually from its architecture, occurrence, and context; follow a plant's natural profile as closely as possible. Take interest in association as plants with analogous tendencies tend to occur together. The more you deviate from this natural machine, the more likely you are to consume resources needlessly or engage in constant series of failed experiments. If you live in a dry, high elevation garden, be realistic about how little water is available on average for plants to succeed. Conversely, if you live in a maritime climate, understand that the inundating presence of rainfall at peak times of the year will strongly limit the plant palette to species that can handle the extreme, even if some seasons are drier. Be honest about your circumstances.

These insights into the habitats and behaviors of plants in local microclimates mirror the kinds of experiences you and I enjoy with plants in gardens. Through a collection of observations, it's easy to pick up on the microclimates in your home landscape: the wet spot near the downspout or the dry woodland slope behind the house. Understanding these subtleties of place can help you match plants with natural adaptations to those conditions. In essence you're planting garden habitats inspired by wild ones with consideration for everything from soils to exposure to climate. Achieving a sense of place comes not only from specific plant choices but placing them in gardens so that they might achieve their full potential.

### Build gardens from native plant foundations and with ample floral diversity, even if some of that diversity isn't native

A functional garden has some ability to self-perpetuate and regenerate as a natural system would and to support life across a variety of trophic levels. If you want a garden with some functional capacity of its own that's resonant with place, building it from a strong foundation of native flora is crucial. Rely on native trees and shrubs for the more enduring features of the landscape because over the course of their lifespans they can support outsized numbers of species in comparison to herbaceous perennials. Woody plants support insects and small mammals even when they decline or die, leaving behind cavities or decaying material that provide nesting and sheltering sites. By supporting diversity of life both in the canopy and understory, native trees and shrubs make positive, long-term contributions to the ecology of place.

Of course, through the lens of supporting local biodiversity, native flora seems a logical food supply for native fauna adapted to local offerings. Several studies of native bees suggest that it only takes eight or more species of native plants to increase abundance and diversity. Yet humans don't eat or thrive on only indigenous foods (and if we did, our diets would be considerably less diverse or balanced). Recent research highlights that planting a three-way cohort of native, near-native, and nonnative plants result in an optimal abundance of floral resources throughout the growing season. Native and near-native plants do a lot of heavy lifting, especially when it comes to supporting larvae. Different species from the same genus, even if they're not native, have been shown to support intermediate

(LEFT) *Quercus* (Oaks) occur throughout the Northern Hemisphere, numbering over 600 species both from temperate and tropical latitudes on four continents. They are often keystone species such as this *Quercus stellata* (post oak) seen growing in this glade and support a multitude of biodiversity.

(BOTTOM) In my front yard meadow, the matrix blurs at times into a colorful and assorted collection of vignettes that has some kind of floral resource present throughout the entire growing season. Everblooming *Prunella vulgaris* (selfheal) and late-summer-flowering *Eragrostis spectabilis* (purple lovegrass) play backup to emergent elements such as *Asclepias tuberosa* (butterfly weed), *A. verticillata* (whorled milkweed), *Hypericum kalmianum* (Kalm's St. John's wort), and *Liatris spicata* 'Trailblazer' (Trailblazer blazing star).

*Aquilegia canadensis* (eastern red columbine) is often found at woodland edges favoring dappled, not direct, exposure and drier soils. Most plant species, though, are far more plastic than we give them credit for. An errant seed found its way to a spot between two conifers in this gravel garden, easily some sixty feet from the nearest possible parent. In more direct light and with no competition, the happy accident is double the size of its likely parents. Sometimes it's worth gardening within the margin of error; serendipity is educational.

numbers of invertebrate diversity. However, nonnative plants play an important supporting role bridging the gaps between different waves of native flora and extend the overall flowering season for foraging adults. This floral choreography is especially important amid climate change as coevolved relationships between pollinators and flowering plants become disrupted and asynchronous. The tumult of climate change affects some organisms more so than others. Bumblebees, in particular, require a season-long supply of floral resources starting in early spring with the ephemeral species with which they've coevolved. Some pollinators are generalists and opportunists, exhibiting low preference toward natives or nonnatives, while others are specialists (such as hoverflies) and require specific plant groups in order to complete their life cycles. In the hybrid landscapes of the modern world, myriad assemblages of plant diversity can form the basis for a thriving web of life. By embracing geographical vicariance of closely related species from similar regions or with similar adaptations to the environment, we can

support biodiversity and create cohesive, richly vegetative gardens. This is surely more desirable than a landscape overrun with a single, dominant, nonnative species doing little in the way to support the vibrancy of local life. Given the challenges facing all of us in the years to come, expanding our views and embracing a bigger picture, even in the footprint of our backyard, can accelerate progress toward beautiful, biodiverse, and resilient landscapes worth living in.

While pollinators may earn headline attention, an array of other, equally important invertebrates benefit from all of this richly vegetated habitat making. Not all insects survive on nectar and pollen; some eat other insects. These natural predators are as important to the balance of the ecosystem as their more gregarious relatives (which are their prey, in some instances). While some plants function as nectar factories, others function as insectaries for rearing thriving populations of natural insect predators such as parasitic wasps, bees, and sawflies. Curiously, members of the aster family (Asteraceae) seem to play an outsized role in supporting these creatures and, given their broad global distribution, underscore the importance of including this diverse lineage in gardens.

Perhaps the best place to find inspiration for this native foundation is in local plant communities or natural spaces near where you live. While you may not enlist this exact palette of plants for your gardening adventure, you'll arrive at powerful ecological insights from the most gregarious species already thriving and performing valuable ecosystem services. In my neighborhood, which surrounds a popular city park along a river, two late-season aster family members grow everywhere—*Symphyotrichum cordifolium* (heartleaf wood aster) and *Rudbeckia triloba* (brown-eyed Susan). Both are available in nurseries, but these local strains likely have a higher degree of specificity for my heavy clay soil. As they show up in the garden, I encourage them to fill voids and rely on them as a natural insurance policy. They also shed insight into the intrinsic worth of members of the aster family, which form a backbone of the midcontinental regional flora. Climatic and environmental insights don't have to limit your planting palette but shed light on those groups and families that have evolved to adapt to your region. Thinking locally may not be the end of the story, but it's a good place to start.

For all that you can learn from local plant communities, the phrase "local is better" deserves some qualification when discussing ecotypes, especially in urban landscapes. An ecotype represents a variant of a species that has adapted to a specific set of local or regional conditions in its wild habitat. These changes may have some minor genetic fingerprint but constitute differences akin to differences in human hair or eye colors. In urban landscapes where soils are historically disturbed or even fundamentally altered, local ecotypes might as well be conscribed to an alien planet. Add to that the microclimates created by engineered infrastructure, and the rigors of urban life can change, hamper, or even prohibit a plant's response to environmental stress. Put simply, local ecotypes may no longer be best equipped for the drastic and accelerated climate change ahead.

The microscale nuances of ecotypes and the provenances from which they come can be valuable in choosing the right plant for the right place and may or may not have any effect on the phenotype of the plant. The oft-bandied adage "right plant, right place" gets a lot of street cred. It's sensical advice—plant with place in mind. But I sometimes wonder just how thoughtfully we understand a plant in order to know whether it's right for the place. Often the circumstances drive the question—given this sandy patch of soil, what plants will grow in sand? While practical and earnest, this question lacks context that could just as well make or break a planting. Reframing it slightly, given this sandy patch of soil in this place, what plants will thrive *here*? In this way, the question strives to understand why plants grow where they do and interpret from that insight a garden of place. A classic example is the documented differences between some provenances of *Asclepias tuberosa* (butterfly weed) based on their adaptation to sand, loam, or clay. Forms from sandy soils do not perform as well in clay as do those adapted to clay soils. While that might seem logical, knowing that a distinction exists is half the battle. Side by side, they're both orange-flowered milkweeds. As for what's happening below the ground, they couldn't be more different.

 # 3   TECHNIQUES FOR MAKING BEAUTIFUL, ECOLOGICALLY VIBRANT GARDENS

**BEFORE PRESENTING** the planting palettes that comprise the rest of this book, let's explore a fundamental and evolving toolbox for gardening on the wild side. These techniques help you apply deeper insights about plants from chapter 1 and the observations of your site from chapter 2 with newfound appreciation. These insights, more guidelines than rules, empower you to let plants take the lead and teach you how to

intervene for the greater legibility of the garden. It's at this juncture that something beautiful, useful, and denser than most gardens we've grown comes into focus. Planting landscapes for today and tomorrow means planting rich communities that form functional wefts of their own, a weave that also includes the thread of our own gardening experience. At first, this sounds incredulous—whatever will plants do if

you're not there to keep them in line? But if you can suspend disbelief that plants can't get along without you, you can start to see the garden as a dynamic system instead of a static assemblage of plants that need individual care as if they were patients in a hospital ward. The landscape on any day is a grand experiment with results we can observe and learn from.

Making an ecological garden is a process conducted over many years without a distinct finish line, a beautiful entanglement with your trowel and the natural world. Beginning with an initial planting, gardening on the wild side is the result of constant evaluation and small changes, a slower sort of gardening that's both pleasureful and powerful. Most importantly, an ecological garden isn't an attempt to recreate some pristine version of nature but, rather, to embrace the nature of the garden itself. Much of this book, especially this chapter, reasserts gardening methods toward more mindful, ecological results.

This isn't to say that a more vibrant, ecological landscape comes from sacrificing a beautiful garden. In some ways, aesthetics are as important as ever, even as New Naturalism relies less on them as the building

My Long Look Prairie is a designed community planted densely to create a biological weft that evokes the natural heritage of the historic grasslands that once covered most of the central United States

Dense plantings are biologically rich, complex, and marvelous; these are the kind of plantings that make good sense in an increasingly turbulent world.

Save for the conifers in the background, nothing in this photo was planted. Yet lacking any human intention, this self-sorting arrangement in its early successional abundance is curious, eclectic, and pleasing. It's also impermanent as many of these taller forbs such as *Silphium perfoliatum* (cup plant) and *Vernonia noveboracensis* (New York ironweed) will quickly outcompete their neighbors in all directions.

blocks of the landscape. By way of analogy, why would we ever let the color of the living room walls determine the construction of the house? Yet historically, that's the unnatural way we've gone about making gardens: imagine a color scheme, pick your favorite plants, or conjure up a theme. Traditionally, a garden was only bounded by human creativity. But what if, instead, we flipped the script and discussed how to plant a garden that works from a sturdy, functional, and site-appropriate foundation upon which we could layer boundless creative thought? While wild nature might be the master, we can pursue a more ecologically conscious gardening that grows harmoniously between our artful yearnings and the nature of place. In this way, a panoply of good planting choices—added up, multiplied, and extrapolated across a landscape—results in the kind of ecologically vibrant, beautiful garden worth living in. This is a garden you want and that works, with more carbon captured, more buzzing and flitting, and an inherent appeal to the curious experiences with wildness we all need more of. This is the kind of garden to spend more time making: one that after some initial effort continues to remake itself.

## EMBRACE THE COLLECTOR'S MINDSET

I want to acknowledge an inherent truth, even if many wouldn't ascribe this to themselves: most gardeners are collectors. At a certain point, we plant what we love and love what we plant. This isn't a bad idea, particularly if we plant things that serve multiple purposes. Intimately knowing and appreciating plants as a gardener-collector lead to deeper connections to the workings of a garden. While we might revel in chartreuse leaves or cobalt blue flowers, every plant is certainly up to something more than just being a pretty face. In the tradition of New Naturalism, a plant collector isn't just hoarding their favorites on a whim, but curating plants that support biodiversity and thrive in place. While certain conditions such as clay soil or environmental variables such as deer overpopulation can at first seem limiting and restricting, they can lead to deep investigations that illuminate opportunities. Embracing a collector's mindset of choosing and acquiring with place and purpose in mind can result in a personal planting palette that's successful, site-specific, and stylish.

In this Irish cottage garden sited on gritty loam, assorted flowers with northern European origins including *Digitalis purpurea* (foxglove), *Leucanthemum vulgare* (oxeye daisy), and *Geranium pretense* (meadow cranesbill) mingle with *Geranium maderense*, a cranesbill native to the island of Madeira. As a result, the planting's palette reflects place and the eclectic nature of this garden.

While principally native to southern Europe, *Narcissus* (daffodils) are beloved throughout the temperate world for their sunny flowers that announce the arrival of spring both in gardens and naturalized settings.

Curating with place in mind is motivated by some interest in plants for what they can do for the garden ecosystem but yields to the realities of the site. For all you might wish to do for your winged friends, the garden actually has to establish and thrive first. Applied to this circumstance, a gardener-turned-curator can take the deep dive into exploring plants that work for a challenging situation. Instead of looking merely at the features of a plant as the motivation for growing it, the suitability of plant to place becomes a winning feature and a recipe for success. As you build a plant-driven repertoire, dabble and experiment, even if it causes short-term design challenges. Give yourself permission to learn from the experience of growing plants and watching them interact and respond to place.

I believe all gardeners carry with them an original flora, if even only in memory. An original flora is comprised of the plants that formed our seminal experiences with gardens and landscapes. This horticultural form of nostalgia could come from anywhere and reveals much about our cultural upbringing and interests. For some gardeners, it's the memory of a plant from childhood. For others, it's the pass-alongs

shared between generations and revered as heirlooms, never left behind in a move or lost from the family, perhaps even bearing a special name to track their origins. These memories inform the plants we often feel the need to grow, an anthropogenic compass that may or may not relate exactly to the place we find ourselves. It's important to cultivate this personal, abiding connection to the land. The collector's mindset is predisposed to this intimate view of plants curated as a palette for making gardens, a kind of grocery shopping list before making dinner. Regardless of the recipe, ingredients matter.

## ORGANIZING THE PALETTE: HORTICULTURAL LAYERS INSPIRED BY NATURE

Great gardens require great plants, but knowing what to do with them is as important as choosing the right plant for the right place. Wild plant communities reveal visual patterns in space for how plants interact together and how they respond to environmental

A globally sourced palette of clump-forming plants including *Allium lusitanicum* 'Summer Beauty' (Summer Beauty ornamental onion), *Ruellia humilis* (wild petunia), *Calamintha nepeta*, and *Sporobolus heterolepis* (prairie dropseed) closed the gaps within three years of planting this designed meadow. Planting design by Jeff Epping.

processes. Throughout this section, I'll translate and glean insights from natural systems for how to combine plants given the conditions we have. In the garden, as in the wild, plants reflect site conditions including soil type, topography, aspect, climate, and ultimately our gardening activity. As a sum of their parts, plant communities are also dynamic, exhibiting change within a single growing season, between any two growing seasons, and over the long-term. For a designed plant community of the greatest integrity, it's important to match plants to the ecological conditions of the site and relate them to one another in a way that ensures their success.

If you sliced through the complex, three-dimensional schematic of wild plant communities, you could articulate a series of layers in which plants grow. The three layers I present in the following sections of this chapter—the matrix layer, the structure layer, and the vignette layer—are archetypal and form a typological theme used in each of the planting palette chapters. While horticulturally conceived, these layers are distilled from observation of natural plant communities, represent niches for plants to occupy, and form a blueprint for the three-dimensional schematic garden. As we discussed in chapter 1, plants occupy niches based

on their unique abilities to exploit available resources and complete their life cycles. These plant lifestyles are genetic and, when understood, are the linchpins for success. Remember that plants don't read books as we do, and this system isn't written into natural law. These layers are meant to help you organize plants, but that doesn't mean some plants can't exist or function in multiple niches or layers.

This approach to combining plants certainly doesn't limit creative expression, but it does ground the plantings in science without having to keep track of all the subjective rules of design. Thus, these layers provide a guide for organizing and assembling plantings into legible and often repeatable guilds that form the basis of beautiful, thriving plant communities. They also form a common language for comparing planting palettes between different areas of your landscape. With some nuances lost to generalization, you can take liberties with these models and tailor them to your garden and site. You should know at this point there are no mistakes in wilder plantings; rather, there are only lessons learned. Some lessons are worth repeating. Some are worth learning never to repeat. Don't expect the police of prudent horticulture to haul you away for your shortcomings or deputize you for your successes.

## The Matrix Layer

The "matrix" is the underlayment of a planting scheme, the green weft that ties everything together. Some authors use this word to describe a particular style of design, but in reality, every wild plant community features a critical ground layer that comprises the majority of vegetation and that often goes unnoticed when up against showier, more overt species. This also grounds the term in some ecological reality—to use a few plants as grout between the tiles requires them to have some ability to perform well in the gaps left between other plants. Plants of this layer, both herbaceous and woody, have low habits, prevent soil erosion, and withstand shade and overhead competition from surrounding companions. They often spread by self-sowing or vegetatively by stolons or rhizomes.

In the woody realm, think of the spreading evergreen stems of *Arctostaphylos uva-ursi* (kinnikinnick) or *Juniperus horizontalis* (creeping juniper), which often inhabit stressful, exposed sites that support limited plant diversity and persist for decades due to their ability to tolerate stress. Low-growing deciduous shrubs such as *Stephanandra incisa* (cutleaf stephanandra) and *Genista lydia* (Lydian broom) similarly thrive in lean soils and do double duty as structural masses that exclude light and cover ground. The herbaceous palette for the matrix layer is substantial, featuring plants with clonal, grasslike growth habits such as *Carex* (sedge) and *Liriope* (lilyturf), or species that form tussocks such as *Sporobolus heterolepis* (prairie dropseed) and *Molinia* (moorgrass), or mats of fine leaves such as *Sedum* (stonecrop) and *Muehlenbeckia* (wire vine). In stressful environments such as coastal regions and deserts, mounded architecture becomes a geometric and functional feature of an otherwise harsh landscape with a unique palette—think of the fuzzy, gray-leaved plants of the Mediterranean including species of *Phlomis* (lampwick plant) and *Helichrysum italicum* (curry plant). While covering ground, these plants also become quite structural too.

Many matrix plants tend to have seasonally dynamic life cycles, reaching peak performance at opportune

Clump-forming perennials with tight rosettes of leaves or clustered crowns also feature in matrix layers provided individual plants cover enough ground and persist through critical periods, such as some species of *Geranium* (cranesbill) (pictured), *Primula* (primrose), or *Sanguisorba officinalis* (burnet).

moments only to fade into the background when conditions change. These don't preclude a plant's functional capacity, but rather define how they function in the context of the planting. For example, in a continental climate with distinct seasons, cool-season perennials reach peak biological activity when temperatures are cool and days are short, emerging to work ahead of most of the planting by prohibiting weedy invaders from germinating at first opportunity. As taller, warm-season perennials become the focal point both biologically and aesthetically, cool-season perennials assume a lesser role and, with proper selection, don't detract from the design.

Consider this layer of ground-covering plants first when designing a new planting, even though it's one of the last layers you'll install. While it's easy to overlook or put off, this critical foundation works hard for the overall integrity of the planting. The absence of this layer, often unsuccessfully replaced by mulches in traditional gardens, results in backbreaking and tedious chores such as mulching and constant weeding. Why not put plants to work instead?

The matrix layer of the landscape often requires more plants than you might think. A labor force requires solid numbers to get the job done right, and the

matrix of a planting scheme is no exception. In native temperate grasslands, plants of this sort can comprise upward of 75 percent of the overall vegetation present in the plant community, which isn't exactly inspiring if all they are is merely green despite their otherwise admirable work ethic. But remember, just because a plant *isn't* included in this layer in your planning doesn't mean it won't contribute to the general cause of covering the ground densely with plants. With some clever accounting, you can safely assume that no less than 40 to 50 percent of the planting should include plants whose primary role is to cover the ground and fill gaps, whether they do anything explicitly ornamental or not. The specifics depend on plants and site, of course, but as a guideline, it's a reasonable place to start, even as it's almost incredulous to think that 50 percent of a planting should include plants that may or may not have anything ornamental about them. But why not? Bare, visible mulch between plants isn't doing much for the garden's aesthetic or contributing to its ecological vibrance. In many cases, these unsung heroes can save you time while providing habitat and cover for wildlife and keeping the garden filled to the brim with lush and exuberant growth.

(TOP) *Iris delavayi* and *I. chrysographes*, both Sino-Siberian irises, function as a matrix in conjunction with *Primula japonica* hybrids. The stiffly upright, structurally valuable blades of these irises contrast with the ground-hugging rosettes of the primroses to form a continuous series of interlocking vegetation that floats between the structural frames of *Rhododendron* and other perennials in this Canadian maritime garden.

(TOP) Two competitive, cool-season perennials—*Carex sprengelii* (Sprengel's sedge) and *Onoclea sensibilis* (sensitive fern)—intersect in a wet meadow planting with *Hyacinthoides hispanica* 'Excelsior' (Spanish bluebells). This dense weft of vegetation does a superb job of excluding unwanted weeds and absorbing runoff.

(BOTTOM) Robust and floriferous, *Prunella vulgaris* (self-heal) comes in a spectrum of colors, blue to pink to white, and forms dense mounds that fill voids between other plants. Like many matrix plants, it perpetuates through reseeding and is particularly suited for poor, compacted, moist soils.

## The Structure Layer

Structural plants give the garden its form, whether the plants form true wood or not. It's easy to think that the only plants to scaffold a garden are those with twigs, branches, and overhanging limbs. But this layer can be quite diverse, both visually and botanically. Woody plants like trees and shrubs are best planted to frame views, while coarse herbaceous plants can provide critical infrastructure within those frames. Given the heavy lifting asked of them, choosing structural plants is no haphazard task. They often persist the longest and exert influence for years after they've established. In this way, you might not realize the contributions of structural plants immediately, so it's always wise to plant with the future in mind. You've likely observed the classic horticultural crime, a case of best intentions, where trees or shrubs were planted too closely

to a home. It's the clearest example of underestimating plants' reality: they grow. Sometimes the best adjudication is simply to remove the perpetrator and start fresh without committing further crimes with a hedge trimmer or chainsaw.

For gardens that require a canopy, trees and shrubs with multiple seasons of interest give gardeners the most return on their investment, especially if planted

(TOP) It's important to understand successional change and embrace it when possible. These *Juniperus virginiana* 'Grey Owl' (Grey Owl red cedars) in a decade will grow into proper shrubs about 6 feet (1.8 meters) tall and 10 feet (3 meters) wide. In this photo, taken in their juvenile stage, they form a low structural mass reminiscent of a matrix plant. They will either need to be removed or severely pruned to keep them in scale with their herbaceous associates.

*Rhus typhina* (staghorn sumac), beloved by many wildlife for its fruits, makes for a light-penetrating scaffold in open and edge environments where its open canopy allows intermingling with herbaceous perennials. Members of the genus *Rhus* (sumac), shrubs and small trees of East Asia, Africa, and North America, often form extensive, competitive copses or colonies that position them to establish early and in abundance in wild plant communities.

A troupe of *Yucca rostrata* in the entry plaza at Denver Botanic Gardens exert themselves on the scene, while a looser matrix of ruderals such as *Nassella tenuissima* (Mexican feather grass), *Eschscholzia californica* (California poppy), and *Centranthus ruber* (Jupiter's beard) scamper underneath.

in a woodland or woodland edge setting. Take willows for instance. Most are shrubs, although a few reach towering proportions. From the breaking of their characteristically fuzzy buds to their soft, sketched shapes at the apex of the growing season to the warm colors of their autumn leaves, most willows offer at least three seasons of horticultural value. Each of these stages has an accompanying ecological contribution—pollen for early pollinators, nesting material, and habitat for birds. Mainstay plants with much to offer carry the garden through the calendar even after the growing season ends. A little goes a long way with plants principally chosen for their skeletal canopies (lest you want to plant a forest from scratch), particularly if they are planted at appropriate spacings that allow them to reach their full potential. In these instances, you might only use structural plants for 5 to 10 percent of the total planting.

But what about plantings in open settings where there's little need for the trunk of a tree or the copse of a shrub? This is where structural herbaceous perennials come in, arguably a category with ascendant popularity thanks to their growing use in contemporary planting schemes. While color is alluring and addicting, form and texture remain long after flowers have faded. In this way, choosing plants for plantings that have persistent features such as colorful or attractive leaves, unique plant habits, or beautiful seedheads make for richer and more enduring garden scenes. It's hard to toss around guidelines with so little specificity, but, in general, the greater the number of features any plant contributes to the planting, the more valuable it is visually and ecologically. Put another way, look beyond showy flowers and consider what else a plant offers for the most horticultural mileage.

In tropical climates, a coarse and luscious palette dominates the horticultural aesthetic as shown at Suan Unyamanee, a private garden and nursery in Thailand. Not only is this signature texture in harmony with the adjacent landscape, it creates a dense and paradisiacal environment for humans and garden creatures.

## The Vignettes Layer

Vignettes are the pretty pictures within a planting, the memories we most often associate with gardens, and the experiences of being in them. Because of this heightened emotional appeal, vignettes and the plant combinations that comprise them are the most consuming and tempting aspects of plantings at the expense of thinking about how to make them thrive. Take the grand and elegant mixed borders of classic gardening books, which are really just a never-ending series of vignettes, permutated and blended into a riot of color and texture. The best of them live on in photos as masterpieces. These purely ornamental gardens would seem to disregard how plants actually grow and evolve for the sake of a beautiful picture. In the end, they exist on life support and require a gardener to keep the picture in the frame. Step away for too long and this eclectic cast could rightly become a choir rehearsal only of soloists, clamoring for the spotlight and inevitably outdoing one another to the end. Yet it is possible to plant a diverse and productive garden that grows in a way that remains sensitive to aesthetics, particularly given a few guidelines to curate both horticulturally and ecologically harmonious combinations.

Vignettes are the content within the frames created by structural plants, often occupying 30 to 50 percent of the design. If structural plants impart some rigidity and permanence to a planting scheme, plants of vignettes soften those lines with looser shapes. Think about the gauzy, diaphanous effect of *Gaura* (wandflower) or the cotton candy clouds of *Muhlenbergia capillaris* (pink muhly). While beautiful, that airy, open canopy allows light to penetrate into the lower layers and encourages adjacent companions to fill in alongside them. While you might get decent mileage from plants such as *Gaura* and *Muhlenbergia*, any plant chosen for this layer could have either a relatively brief or extended bloom season, the particulars of which are only important for how they interact alongside their neighbors and contribute to the visual result. The smallest gardens tend to result in more composed plantings simply due to a lack of space for more complex patterns, but they can still do so without sacrificing their functional benefits. This compositional strategy becomes more tedious at scale without some overriding functional theme. With larger plantings, each planting layer becomes integral to the effectiveness of the horticultural machine.

Vignettes can also arise from softer integrations of plants within a matrix, even if serendipitously so. These finer scale combinations are more impactful upon close inspection, providing the intimate details that make a garden imaginative, personal, and unique. At scale, they blur into one or more adjacent layers, but can do so without overpowering a planting or making it visually excessive. Regardless of how they come together, vignettes should be dynamic because they carry the garden throughout the season from one flowering event to another.

Plants for vignettes can flower ad nauseam if you're keen on something hanging around for half the summer. While there's nothing wrong with floriferous output, permanency can lead to a plant becoming less interesting. Been there, seen that. Some plants with more seasonal charisma—such as irises in spring or *Hibiscus* in late summer—have an emblematic personality; they define the season in which they flower with chronological panache. A garden without these seasonal pacesetters can lack rhythm and start to look more like the mass-produced landscapes of the commercial world than the kinds of lovingly crafted creations better suited for home. Using emblems in concert with plants with longer seasons of interest help to diversify the garden with a succession of interest and an abundance of floral resources for insects and birds.

Bulbs might be the best and most familiar example of emblematic plants. Given their biology, plants that grow from bulbs often exhibit ephemeral characteristics, arising and completing their life cycle amid favorable conditions only to return to dormancy thereafter. The cadence of spring-flowering bulbs such as daffodils and tulips makes for great horticultural theater, the glitzy kind of production that makes a garden

(TOP) An annual species of *Dichanthelium* (a selection of which is often sold as *Panicum* 'Frosted Explosion'), plays the part of haze in a complex planting scheme. As an undercurrent to showier, floral elements, its loose and pendulous panicles float through the mid-level of the planting, occupying a critical gap easily intruded by unwanted weeds. Left to seed, it can lightly intersperse itself in a ruderal fashion, taking advantage of gaps as they open throughout the scheme.

(LEFT) In wet, productive soils, as in this border along a stream at Mount Usher near Ashford, Ireland, clumping species such as white *Astilbe*, *Hosta*, and *Iris ensata* (Japanese iris) form a continuous ribbon of leafy crowns while churning out flowers overhead. Reseeding colonies of *Primula japonica* (Japanese primrose) fill gaps with tight rosettes of foliage that give rise to delicate flowers for a headliner display in late spring.

Bijou and bejeweled, this planting features myriad annual flowers in eclectic colors and shapes; it's spring fever before summertime. The grassy strands are the emergent leaves of *Muhlenbergia capillaris* (pink muhly), which will surge over the planting as the seasonal tide rolls on, an ecological choreography considerate of aesthetics.

seem glamorous, if only for a moment. Maybe most of all, they celebrate seasonality, something to which our Western style seems increasingly numb. While architecture and structure might give a planting character, richly planted vignettes replete with seasonal emblems give a garden depth. For the creatures we share the garden with, they ensure a steady stream of biological activity from the stirring buds of *Trillium* in the woodland garden to the final puff of aster seeds in the open meadow. Emblems also contribute to the garden ecosystem, particularly when they emerge quickly and form semi-persistent foliage such as *Podophyllum* (mayapples), closing early-season gaps created by still-dormant perennials.

With all this attention on floral dynamics and acrobatics, it's easy to develop a little pride for the success that comes along the way. Yet of any of the major planting layers articulated in this book, this is perhaps the most fleeting. Admittedly, structural plants keep growing and can shift or alter the frame of the garden over time, but vignettes evolve on account of more diversity. While some species might persist for decades, as some certainly should for the stability of the planting, others will come and go, perhaps only to return for a moment from the seedbank in light of disturbance. You might choose to include these plants as the life of the party just to keep the garden interesting, while more staid elements grow into their own. Change in gardening is inevitable, if not also a good thing. That said, when embracing ruderality and ephemerality, don't commit to more than 5 to 10 percent of the planting to species or varieties with these traits lest you enslave yourself to their constant tending. As with opportunistic plants in general, they may flourish initially absent competition, but will likely succumb to the shade and pressures of nearby, longer-lived plants.

(RIGHT) In plantsman Jimi Blake's backyard meadow in County Wicklow, Ireland, *Gladiolus communis* var. *byzantinus* (common corn-flag) and *Allium* 'Purple Rain' reach a summer apex amid a matrix of native grasses and *Ranunculus acris* (meadow buttercup) before the community retires for the rest of the growing season.

(OPPOSITE PAGE) *Narcissus* 'Stint' fills a critical seasonal vacancy between clumps of *Carex appalachica* (Appalachian sedge) in this meadow matrix, juxtaposed in dramatic fashion against the emergent leaves of *Penstemon digitalis* 'Dark Towers' (Dark Towers beardtongue).

This vignette invites intimate inspection, a horticultural three-part harmony featuring subtle contrasts among *Heuchera macrorhiza* 'Autumn Bride' (Autumn Bride coral bells), *Persicaria amplexicaulis* 'Firetail' (Firetail mountain fleece), and *Patrinia scabiosifolia* 'Nagoya' (Nagoya golden lace). While all three present their flowers on lithe, sinuous stems, the nuances of their flower shapes—spike versus umbel-cyme versus tiny bells—with leafy interjections make for a dynamic bouquet of perennials that flower for weeks in the heat of summer.

*Echinacea pallida* (pale purple coneflower) and *Allium sphaerocephalon* (drumstick allium) roll with a spherical beat in stark relief to the spiky textures of *Verbascum chaixii* 'Album' (nettle-leaved mullein) and pink-violet *Astilbe* in the background. The combo is ecologically sympatico–*Verbascum* and *Echinacea* (rosettes) form tight circles between which *Allium* (strappy stems) emerge and *Penstemon barbatus* (amorphous mounds) color in the difference. Planting design by Piet Oudolf at Kew Gardens (London, UK).

## Kitschy Plants

*Datisca cannabina* (false hemp) elicits a range of responses when first encountered in the garden—the hallmark of the ultimate kitsch plant. This Cretan and Turkish native with an understated yet structural personality fixes nitrogen, making it easily adaptable to a variety of soil conditions.

As a final nod to those who truly garden as an expression of their own style and taste, I find gardens so much more engaging when a gardener dives in with a truly offbeat planting scheme. With so many plants in the world from which to choose, and a great deal of them unused, planting adventurously can open doors to new ways of thinking. If you want a truly authentic planting, it's worth tapping your personal and local palettes whenever possible. These plants—at once kitschy, beatnik, or local color—add character and personality and may not be found abundantly in nature or in commerce. Consider the freeform, curious personalities of plants such as *Phytolacca* spp. (pokeweed) and *Datisca cannabina* (false hemp) or the head-turning prowess of a *Crinum* (crinum lily) or *Cypripedium* (ladyslipper orchid), all of which can seem entirely unexpected.

## Assembling Plant Communities for Resilient Results

Assembling plant communities is perhaps the principle function of garden-making in the New Naturalism tradition; this is where the fun begins. A designed plant community is a dynamic combination of plants inspired by the ecological idea that many different species coexist in and respond to similar environmental conditions and one another. Despite widespread adoption of the idea in this book, the science of plant communities is highly complex and interpretable. One rule seems clear: any plant community occurs as a sum of plants filling niches. Each species occurs in response both to prevailing site conditions and in response to the competitive environment created by its associates. By applying our understanding of plants, their biology, and architecture, we can fashion beautiful and functional combinations.

Any rule in gardening should be broken at least once in an effort to learn if it were truly a good idea in the first place. It may have merely been a guideline.

In a medium as fickle as planting design, it's hard to imagine too many rules about ordering plants together in a space that holds steadfast and true across all conditions. All that being said, these so-called assembly rules amount to good advice from one gardener to another for how to apply plants to the ground and relate them to one another with an eye for style and practicality. A great many more techniques remain undiscovered. As gardeners, this opens up a vast array of creative possibilities for bringing together plants from different geographies but with similar ecological profiles toward the most resilient gardens possible. With an assessment of site and some understanding of the niches plants occupy, you can begin to assemble beautiful, resilient plant communities with a layered palette by relating plants to place and one another. As the garden

This designed plant community around a small water garden features a densely planted, site-specific, and regionally relevant palette. Water is both a constituent of the community's structure and a condition of the site.

evolves, you'll no doubt discover artful and creative opportunities for planting as the plant community responds to the site, potentially revealing new niches and serendipitous combinations.

Depending on the size of your garden, these designed plant communities might become as elaborate as garden habitats, the sum of many similar or thematic communities varied over time and space. In smaller gardens, these landscape-level patterns are hard to perceive, much less render or understand. Your garden becomes a part of the bigger fabric of the neighborhood or environment around you. The frames of the spaces you've imagined throughout your study of place provide a more finite and accessible means of creating plant communities scaled to the realities of the home garden. While your exact approach might not mirror a purely wild precedent, the nature of plants together under similar conditions even in a small space creates something dynamic that makes gardens of this approach so fascinating and important to the future of the planet.

### Plant redundantly within and among layers for the greatest ecological abundance possible

Plants that share a common evolutionary heritage often function and perform similarly in their communities, meaning, two species in the same genus in the same community are more likely to be similar than two species from different genera, even if they have evolved in different regions. Think of these two goldenrods as cousins; one is American, *Solidago speciosa* and the other is European, *Solidago virgaurea.*

Within each of the three layers introduced in the previous section, it's important to recall one of nature's principle lessons: redundancy is a good thing. Few wild plant communities contain only one plant doing a particular job in any given layer, often because an array of microclimates exists as a result of variations in site conditions and the interactions among plants. As in a large company, for each role there are often several positions to fill, particularly at the mid- and lower levels of the employment hierarchy. Plant communities have similar hierarchies. This explains why

the number of species of *Carex* (sedge) can number in the tens or dozens in many wild communities where they occur. While they are functionally redundant and certainly visually similar, they work as a cohort, filling all the available niches in their given layer. If one or a few species fall out of the mix, the system responds by reassigning others to cover the tasks. This kind of abundance is often severely lacking if not totally absent in traditional gardens, which partly explains the amount of time and energy required to artificially fill the voids either by mechanically removing weeds or constantly intervening to control plant growth. Mastering the subtleties of abundance and site might sound like a game of nuances, but it represents an important insight about plant communities both wild and designed: plants eventually fill all the niches available.

Increasing abundance starts to move garden-level plant diversity toward a resilient reality. If all species in the garden behave similarly, even under the same conditions, a single disturbance event such as a drought or a flood could decimate the planting. Like a good investment strategy, diversity is good for the health of the portfolio. Some plant populations will expand or diminish, but the net result will be persistent and stable. But diversity, as we've learned, isn't created equal—the details matter. Plantings with more evenly distributed functional traits will tend to flourish in comparison to those with less, even when species richness is higher. But without splitting hairs, it's fair to say that with a greater array of plants in your garden, the better your chances will be for a more functional and stable community over time.

The sum total of all this social profiling is this: planting from across the functional strategies described in chapter 1 and applied to the layers presented in this chapter can result in a richer, self-perpetuating garden, a true community of interrelated individuals that function as a cohort. In small gardens, the garden's size dictates that each planting choice performs a greater number of functions relative to a bigger plot. This just makes planting choice ever more critical.

You'll likely end up choosing plants that don't fit so discretely into the function of a single layer. In this

(TOP LEFT) *Solidago speciosa* (American goldenrod).

(TOP RIGHT) *Solidago virgaurea* (European goldenrod).

(LEFT) The art of gardening isn't in the static control of specific textures, colors, or combinations but is instead in an assembled palette rich with traits that flourish and thrive over time despite nature's curveballs. The fact that these *Liatris pycnostachya* (prairie blazing star) steal the show in August is merely a bonus—they earn their keep from having colonized a wet spot in this planting where few other plants in the community would thrive.

Even in a border just over 6 feet (1.8 meters) in depth, this planting at Bodnant Gardens in Wales is a riot of interest because of its abundant diversity. In every functional niche, multiple species succeed to functional and aesthetic standards.

realm of horticultural multitasking, it's important to appreciate plants for their beauty and function in all seasons, even outside of traditional ornamental definitions. You might include hefty, skyward perennials such as *Eupatorium* (Joe-Pye weed) or *Dahlia* for their structural heft, but admittedly we think of them first for their flowers. Comparatively, ground-covering perennials such as *Prunella* (self-heal) and *Thymus* (thyme) flower off and on for months while dutifully excluding light from reaching the soil surface with tidy, vegetative mats. Late-flowering perennials such as *Chrysanthemum* don't have much to say until the growing season is nearly over but emerge early and persist as spreading clumps in the matrix layer. This cross-functional environment gives you some cover downstream when the garden may require a bit of direction. If you have more than enough plants performing the same function, editing becomes easy with precise acts of shovel pruning.

Abundance has limits in a smaller garden, which might support fewer species in a self-perpetuating fashion simply as a function of space—you can only cram so many plants into a given area. But the richness is relative: a small garden can still support more plant diversity than a traditional hedge and an evergreen groundcover. For the sake of prescription, I wish it were easy to prescribe levels of abundance within any given layer. As a reference, in the wild, the matrix layer often contains the most species abundance, if not also the most plants. Plants of the matrix cover the most space as they intercalate the gaps between everything else. In gardens, we might favor a little less diversity just to allow plants in other niches, but if we throttle it entirely, we'll end up with a garden that requires more life support than not. Structural plants, both woody and herbaceous, often occur at low to intermediate levels of abundance in the wild and might in the garden, too, depending on the design. Too many of these might result in a monoculture or patch of low diversity with time (in which case, if that's the goal, plant onward). In the vignette layer, any type of plant will likely occur at low to intermediate levels of abundance and only at the higher end of the spectrum for those constituting

While the *Tradescantia* hybrid (spiderwort) proliferates both via runners and seeds, it hasn't yet outcompeted the dense crowns of *Nepeta faassenii* 'Purrsian Blue' (Purrsian Blue catmint). The more ruderal *Silene vulgaris* (bladder campion) moves around in relationship to both competitors always finding a gap to call home. Later in summer, warm-season grasses *Eragrostis trichodes* (sand lovegrass) and *Bouteloua* 'Blonde Ambition' (Blonde Ambition blue grama grass) close over the edges of this gravel garden floral vignette.

a strong visual or seasonal theme. From here you have artistic license, but only to the extent that choices are ecologically compatible with the site, an idea explored further in the next section.

### Plantings have to be ecologically compatible to thrive vibrantly

Once you've measured the ingredients, how do you go about putting them together? A good baker knows how precise a perfect chocolate cake recipe is due to the ordering of dry ingredients, wet ingredients, and careful mixing. Planting schemes on the wild side deserve this kind of careful composition: measured, intended, and blended. You can't simply compose schemes of plants that only look good together if they

In this generous border between a bunkhouse and small pond, water-loving perennials form a lush, competitive, and architectural community. *Astilbe* 'Purpur-lanze,' *Rodgersia pinnata* 'Superba,' and *Actaea* 'Black Negligee' thrive along this wet edge between woods and meadow in a matrix of *Deschampsia cespitosa* 'Goldtau' (Gold Dew tufted hair grass). Planting design by Tony Spencer.

don't also relate to one another ecologically; it's essential to cover the ground horizontally and vertically with vegetation—no gaps, please. You have to plant artful arrangements based on plants' social tendencies and survival strategies as described in chapter 1. Competition is the first survival strategy to account for in order to ensure that one or two species don't overrun the whole garden. Any two plants growing together should be able to coexist without constant meddling or coddling, provided you've considered whether they were competing directly for resources at the same time. Intuitively, you wouldn't likely plant a vigorous runner

(LEFT) In Beth Chatto's gravel garden, a cloudlike matrix of *Pennisetum villosum* (silky fountaingrass) and *Nassella tenuissima* (Mexican feather grass) hold together soft, amorphous mounds of drought-tolerant perennials and bulbs that hail from similar habitats around the world such as *Verbascum*, *Nepeta* spp., *Helianthemum* 'Cheviot,' *Allium sphaerocephalon* (drumstick onion), and *Verbena rigida* (stiff vervain).

(LEFT) The nature of these conditions promotes a mind-boggling number of species that thrive in harmony because the site's limited fertility and environmental stress prohibit any plant species from becoming dominant.

(OPPOSITE PAGE) Ephemeral, spring-flowering plants such as this *Allium christophii* (star of Persia) integrate well in plantings that can disguise their inevitable return to dormancy. In this lush spring vignette, almost all plants in the ground layer will transition out of the picture by midsummer in favor of perennials that had only barely emerged at the time this photo was taken. Dense planting works because of the choreographed layers of plants that come in and out of view throughout the growing season.

In this vignette, warm-season grasses such as *Sporobolus heterolepis* (prairie dropseed), various *Carex* (sedge, and *Molinia* (moorgrass) cultivars form a fine matrix through which other patchy colonies of perennials emerge, including *Helenium autumnale* 'Bandera' (Mariachi™ Bandera Helen's flower) and *Penstemon digitalis* 'Dark Towers' (Dark Towers beardtongue). Ruderals such as *Lobelia cardinalis* (cardinal flower) fill early successional gaps. As the planting aged, these gaps closed and the cardinal flower disappeared within a few seasons.

next to a slow-growing clumper. Haphazardly jamming a bunch of plants together may produce a competitive result, but not an aesthetic or resilient one.

But let's not forget a plant's ability to withstand stress and respond to disturbance. Stress throttles the proliferation of the most aggressive species, whether they spread from seed or by other vegetative means. Stress becomes something of an equalizer, favoring plants that can withstand it and working against those that require more favorable conditions. Stress can refer to a litany of environmental stressors ranging from drought to flooding, variations in fertility, and lack of soil oxygen. Disturbance is anything that destroys biomass that's already been produced, like a deer munching off the new growth on your favorite shrub. Human or animal foot traffic, severe weather events, changes to the soil horizons, and seasonal mowing are all forms of disturbance that can affect home gardens. Reading between the lines, you could infer that general gardening activities such as planting and weeding could constitute as disturbance, which is entirely accurate, if not also something to be aware of.

The approach outlined here for planting abundant layers of plants considers both phenology (when plants flower) and physiology (how and when plants grow). Spacing plants and arranging them in patterns within the respective layers varies based on how productive and stressful the site is, something you've learned from your assessment of place. The relationships between these two variables create an almost innumerable range of planting conditions around the world.

**Environments with less stress and greater productivity** feature stable growing conditions, readily available soil moisture, and fertility. These sites favor plants that can convert those rich resources into biomass, especially those that form extensive colonies, large crowns, or attain significant size in a single growing season. In open exposures, plants often have bold textures and high degrees of greenness, which will factor into your design. The goal of your planting will determine if you prefer more competitive plants to cover a large area quickly or if you eliminate those

entirely so as to minimize the chances of one or a few completely dominating the planting. Choose **matrix** species with competitive and likely shade-tolerant profiles as they will secede to taller plants later in the season. Larger groupings in the **matrix** and **vignettes** layer will most closely match those with coarse, architectural social profiles. Plants that proliferate under high fertility such as grasses will quickly fill the space after planting.

**Environments with greater stress and less productivity** are often xeric or partially so for extended times throughout the growing season and have soils with relatively low fertility. Plants that thrive in these conditions have generally conservative growth habits, occupy specific niches, or persist with resilient above- and belowground architectures. Sites of this nature have the opportunity to support broad assemblages of plant diversity so long as they can grow leanly. **Matrix** species should generally be long-lived with low architectures that cover the ground closely or fill spaces

between other plants. **Structural** species ideally will have some drought tolerance, if environmental stress is related to lack of moisture. The **vignettes** layer could feature an array of diversity intermixed to form strong seasonal patterns of 3 to 6 species in flower at any one time.

**Environments between these conditions** result in a visual pattern of a series of isolated, patchy groups or solitary individuals—in other words, relatively lower degrees of sociality. The stress of low fertility comes at a net cost to competitive species, reducing growth rates

(TOP) In this traditional ornamental border at Waterperry Gardens (Oxfordshire, UK), a classic cohort of summer-flowering perennials such as *Phlox paniculata* (tall garden phlox), *Achillea ptarmica* 'The Pearl' (The Pearl sneezewort), and *Achillea filipendulina* (fernleaf yarrow) grow densely with occasional intercessions of *Eryngium giganteum* (Miss Willmott's ghost). With the exception of the latter, all have leafy or upright architectures (or both) that shade the ground. The *Eryngium* emerges from a basal rosette in gaps between the others.

and resulting in more persistent gaps in the planting for ruderal species to occur. As a caveat, gardeners might perceive competitive species under stress as unhealthy or performing poorly given rigorous standards of horticultural cultivation; that's a judgment for each and their own.

For example, if you're using a less-competitive plant to dramatic effect, counteract that by using less-aggressive species throughout the planting. You will still want to plant redundantly within each layer to

The famed Lurie Garden (Chicago, IL, USA) famously celebrates the spirit of the prairie which it captures through the use of charismatic local flora such as *Echinacea pallida* (pale purple coneflower) and *Eryngium yuccifolium* (rattlesnake master). These scenes, while artistic by conception, reflect a maxim of landscape ecology: a few species account for most individuals in the community, especially when they're contributing to the visual product. Consequently, if you're adding up the niches and accounting for a handful of dominant players in each season, most species are represented by only a few individuals.

make sure all of the roles in the planting are filled. Openings in woodlands will have assorted textures at the edges, often bolder textures in the understory, and strong biases towards spring flowers, linked to the availability of light permeating through to the understory. Sunny, grassland precedents often feature uniformly fine textures, varying degrees of competition, and densely structured communities that may have seasonally distinctive patterns based on the cool- or warm-season life histories of their constituents.

Ultimately, you have to use and apply the ingredients appropriately. Broadly speaking, I'm most interested in conveying an ecological sense of how to combine plants to enhance any artfulness you already possess for arranging plants in gardens. To borrow a situation from the kitchen, salt will never substitute for cane sugar. But agave nectar, maple syrup, and honey might. How much you use of any of the alternatives might vary a little, but the result is still sweet to some degree. In the garden, if you want to plant 100 of something for dramatic effect, they will only thrive with resilience if they're able to succeed ecologically at that scale in the first place. If you're trying to achieve a result that doesn't require intense management and resources, massing and grouping can't be an arbitrary exercise in aesthetics. Plant selection for any designed community, regardless of type or style, should strive for selections with similar growth habits to promote equitable levels of competition. Greater diversity of plant shapes and growth rates will pay off in the long run as plants respond to site and communities evolve, the visual results of which are discussed later in this chapter. These kinds of long-term fluctuations may change the specific look of a community over time, but just because it looks different doesn't mean it can't, or shouldn't, be held to a beautiful standard.

As you look for inspiration, you'll note several strands of naturalistic planting design, broadly speaking, that have emerged in professional practice in the last few decades in the Western world. These range from plantings that verge on total wildness with only marginal interventions to more artificial, contrived plantings that reference a wild community in spirit.

Where your garden falls on the spectrum is entirely subjective and up to you. In the former strand, many people might not even recognize the result as a garden, even after significant investments of time and plants, because it lacks the coherence required for most to recognize it as a designed space (and instead could lead to it being incorrectly perceived as a wild space). In the latter strand, the aesthetic is inspired by an impression of wildness that results in plantings closer to traditional gardens in their requirements to manage. Regardless of the stylistic varnish you apply, plants in place are never static, so to assume their picturesque permanence is to accept the need for onerous efforts to maintain them or live in constant disillusion. The methods for relating plants to site and to one another require honest acknowledgement of plants' social tendencies.

### To evoke drifts of naturalized color, increase the numbers of plants in larger social groupings

A drift planting pattern is one of the more overt natural patterns of plant distribution, even if it has few empirical delimiters. While it's tempting to invoke a painterly analogy from a purely aesthetic perspective, understanding how a drift forms in nature is more helpful for designing a successful plant community in the garden. In fact, a drift is often perceived as just a mass of plants, when they may be more spatially separated and diverse. We know that some plants disseminate farther than other species on account of their sociable tendencies in a community. Like apples falling from a tree, most of the apples land nearest the base of the trunk. Some roll away a little farther. Others might end up even farther after an animal eats the fruit and sheds the seed. The result is the majority of plants concentrated in one place and with fewer strewn farther from the source. Adopting these patterns underscores another reality of wild plant communities: nature offers few, if any, clean delineations between vegetation. In the garden, this comes as a virtue with more artistic license. By stylizing wild plant communities for greater aesthetic legibility, gardeners can amplify plant groupings for bold visual impact, blurring from one drift to another.

In general, if a plant naturally forms monocultures in a highly sociable fashion, it's a good candidate for large monocultural blocks in plantings. Monocultural blocks are also subject to population-level competitive pressures. For plants that naturally grow in large colonial masses, such as *Monarda* (bee balm) or *Lythrum* (loosestrife), for example, their average growth rate will likely account for any setbacks they experience, an evolved mechanism for dealing with the stress of

While translated from wild origins, these drifts of perennials seem to effortlessly intersect with a robust selection of *Euphorbia schillingii* (Schilling spurge), forming a soft green hedge couched between *Kniphofia* (poker plant) and *Thalictrum* (meadow rue) in a carefully composed color scheme. Planting design by Piet Oudolf.

This dynamic duo illustrates high volume contrast—the finely textured froth of *Eragrostis spectabilis* (purple lovegrass) versus the crisp radial architecture of *Yucca filamentosa* (Adam's needle).

I call this power of 10 planting. If you think 10 of something is a sound number, scale it up by a factor of 10 and you might ultimately get closer to the dream you have in your head. This is especially true of bulbs, which are small and, luckily, fairly inexpensive. This planting of *Eremurus stenophyllus* (foxtail lily) contains many dozens to achieve this effect. Make no small plans, even if you have to invest in them over time.

an occasional setback. For plants not predisposed to colonial growth, horticultural masses might decline over time due to disease or other density-dependent variables resulting from overcrowding.

In the wild, studies suggest that competition between individuals of the same species is more effective than competition between individuals of different species. I established this in chapter 1 in the discussion of competition as a population-based force perceived per individual. In the garden, that often means we have to scale up numbers of plants within groups or masses, instead of the collections of one or a few that we might be inclined to plant. By increasing the masses by factors of three or more times that of traditional plantings, we'll end up with tightly woven patches that have higher degrees of competition between like individuals.

### Contrast everything and don't be afraid to break your pattern

If you take nothing else from this chapter, know that the quickest way to craft visual interest is to dial up contrast. The scalar differences between plants help us recognize and value them—while we take note of loudness first, it can help us appreciate quietness when the volume goes down. When several plants that all look similar dominate a planting scheme, the result is visually indistinguishable. This is why planting redundantly for the purposes of function doesn't often have a consequential result on what the planting looks like. But in order to keep a garden interesting, there have to be clear visual contrasts within and between layers. If you're experimental by nature, you'll have a lot of fun discovering novel, creative schemes worthy of Instagram and all forms of digital bragging. If you're in this for success, take note of a few basic principles of plant architecture from chapter 1, by differing plant

Contrasting floral textures can result in exciting vignettes. The dusty blue orbs of this choice form of *Allium caeruleum* (blue globe onion) create a geometric conversation in stark relief against a low hedged frame and associates such as *Echinacea paradoxa* (yellow coneflower) and *Penstemon cardinalis* (NativeRoots™ cardinal beardtongue).

A well-placed umbel is the mark of a fine gardener or planting designer, a floral shape so different than most that it levitates among its garden companions with seeming effortlessness. *Ammi majus* (bishop's flower) floats between gaps in a rose garden with *Foeniculum vulgare* 'Bronze' and *Verbena bonariensis* (purpletop).

architectures for visual and ecological vibrancy. If you find yourself falling into a habit of using a particular plant feature over and over again, force yourself to break your pattern. This is also true of imitation. The results might just be brilliant.

The English-born scientist, poet, and gardener G.F. Dutton used the simple idea of contrasting horizontal and vertical lines to tame the wildness he gardened marginally in the Scottish Highlands. He employed the use of flat, green, horizontal surfaces such as mown paths to frame vertical colonies of shrubs and tall trees. Beyond aesthetics, this has a functional implication too. Like a natural plant community, the more we can spatially segregate different kinds of competitive plants in a horizontal plane from one another, the more we can promote overall diversity in a plant community by reducing the likelihood of competition between species. In these complex, dense plantings, legibility is critical. While the result might achieve your goals for a lush garden, some plants should stand out prominently, either as large clonal colonies or in strong seasonal themes to preserve a visual understanding throughout the year.

### Keep the design legible and coherent with clear visual interest in all seasons

Regardless of the techniques you've applied to date, never resist the urge to step back, pause, and assess whether your ideas are legible. The discussion of legibility in this chapter dealt with the topic at the scale of the landscape, particularly how to frame spaces for living, movement, and planting. Within a planting, legibility and coherence are equally important. Legibility helps us read the scene (yes, it's a garden). Coherence is about the wholeness and consistency of a design (yes, it's a garden that's beautiful for discernible reasons). The aggregation of individual plants into repeatable units allows our brain to perceive patterns, which form the basis for how we interpret what we see and how we respond to it.

Beauty is in the eye of the beholder, for sure. Some gardeners might disavow naturalistic planting as merely a style with which they just don't jibe. This book seeks to expand that viewpoint, if only to argue that style is but half of the equation, although an important one in recruiting more to practice New Naturalism. Yet for the sake of stylistic conversation, the lack of legibility and coherence are the strongest misgivings among gardeners more accustomed to tidiness and order. As a gardener, this is where passions for colors, textures,

Contrast doesn't have to be drastic or abrupt and can vary gradually across a range of plants. This ruderal planting of reseeding annuals and perennials is fine-textured overall, but each component finds a space to shine, mostly due to a disciplined color palette.

(TOP) Embrace the distraction of color, favoring structure for more visual mileage. While the warm oranges shown here look quite sophisticated, the structure of the grass and the remnant cones both of the *Echinacea* (coneflower) and *Helenium* (sneezeweed) will outlast this moment.

(RIGHT) Planting for features gives you fodder for celebrating seasonal change in the garden. Organizing vignettes around multiple aesthetic and functional themes in a handful of species link the life cycles of plants with the seasons in which they are inherently beautiful.

Never underestimate the power of a well-placed ball on a stick, in this case *Allium sphaerocephalon* (drumstick onion). Verticality combined with strong geometry can never fail, aesthetically speaking. Our eyes just don't expect it.

and forms become valuable. With some traditional fluency in this visual language of plants, you can curate seasonal themes around one or a few ornamental traits that stitch the garden together in some orderly way. By striving for the clearest visual ideas throughout the growing season, you can create a garden that's both beautiful and ecological, a marvelous source of wonderment and awe.

Color theory is as subjective in its application as it is inarguable in its science. The use of color in complex plantings can result in a unique, personal aesthetic, but this topic already earns unparalleled coverage in the gardening and floral design literature (and you've probably already read one or three books on it already). Ample resources exist for developing an eye for color patterns and combinations that you can layer over the functional paradigms explained in this chapter. Above all, embrace color as a distraction and celebrate it as frosting on a good cake; it's easier to fix a colorful smudge than it is to rebake the "cake."

### Make lists and do math

How do you take an eclectic, functional array of plants organized into layers and turn them into a garden? Perhaps the nagging question to address is, how many different kinds of plants to include in a design or even how many units of any given plant should you include? As this chapter outlines, there's no magic formula. Most importantly, regardless of pattern or arrangement, you should assemble a planting to fill all available space. Open space becomes a vacuum and something of a Pandora's Box; you're gambling with the site, its dynamics, and whatever you're planting.

While it's important to visualize relationships between plants, I often find that drawing encumbers home gardeners, nervous about their abilities or committing some error of scale that could result in underplanting or overordering plants (if there ever were such a problem beyond the limitations of your bank account). Presuming you're starting with a blank slate, I often advise gardeners and even professionals first to create a spreadsheet of your planting choices, including columns for seasons of interest,

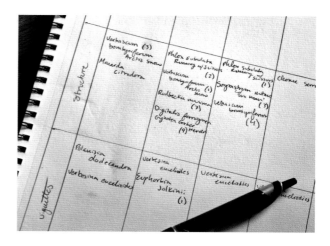

Perhaps even more valuable than a fussy drawing or complicated spreadsheet is a simple table to account for plants utilized in each of the three layers of the designed plant community. You can bend and vary the rules, but this gives you a schematic to begin with and plenty of margins for scribbling and adjusting as you go.

size, architecture or shape, planting layer, and, ultimately, a column for calculating quantities. This can help you visualize in tabular form where your planting schemes might have functional and aesthetic gaps. You can do this in an organized list as well, but a spreadsheet will prove helpful for calculating quantities of plants to apply to the planting area. The spreadsheet or list method distills the planting design process to the assessment and calculation of relationships between plants and their layers.

If you're integrating plants into an existing garden scheme, an organized list of layers to enhance should suffice to help organize your ideas. Often the layer most lacking (or absent altogether) in traditional plantings is the matrix. Thinking about the shapes of existing plants, how much shade they cast on the ground plane, and the overall conditions of the site can quickly define the parameters for plants that would succeed as an underlayment to an existing garden. Structural and vignette layers are often easier to enhance in existing plantings, depending on the scale of the remodeling effort. The fixes here might be reduced to planting individuals or small groups to close gaps and strengthen existing visual or functional relationships.

If your garden or planting space is less than 100 square feet (9.3 square meters), you might be able to do this exercise with just a ruler, pencil, and paper. A common scale to use for drawing detailed planting plans is 1:4 or 4 feet (1.2 meters) of space on the ground for every 1 inch (2.5 cm) drawn on paper. The scale depends on how large or detailed you might want to render a plan; a larger site will require a finer scale, perhaps 1:10 or 10 feet (3 meters) of space on the ground for every 1 inch (2.5 cm) drawn on paper in order to fit it all onto a reasonably sized piece of paper (such as 11 × 17 inches [28 × 43 cm]).

Using the layered typology espoused earlier, I start building spreadsheets and lists by acknowledging that even when spacing plants 6 to 12 inches (15 to 30.5 cm) apart for 100 percent of the available area for the planting, you'll still have gaps when you're done. This is why I often build spreadsheets that "overplant" the available area, sometimes upward of 150 percent. Part of this paradox is inherent in the area calculation of a two-dimensional surface. As the layered typology makes clear, plantings are three-dimensional, which pose a challenge for conceiving them on a flat piece of paper (unless you opt for multiple sheets of paper layered on top of one another, which can be helpful). Plants growing in close confines to one another spread leaves, stems, and flowers as overlapping canopies over the ground, creating dense layers of vegetation like layers of cake and frosting stacked on top of one another. As you'll discover later in this chapter, it's good to be dense.

At a minimum, devise trios of species with similar ecological profiles and different aesthetic variables. Groupings like this can eventually grow to include 5 to 10 or more different kinds of plants as you gain confidence combining them and observing their success over time. In each of these groupings, start with those plants that have the most enduring features throughout the growing season; these keep the garden in order. Add ephemerality last, as if it were sprinkles on top of that frosted cake. This modular method to composing plant communities puts a little more pressure on writing the recipe, so to speak, but makes quick work of executing the planting project. Arranging these in a single tray before taking off with the trowel can alleviate second-guessing and allow you to focus on spacing plants. It's also easy if you have garden helpers who may not have all the finer details of the project committed to memory.

If you're a bit overwhelmed with new information, don't stress. For all the guidelines offered here, it's tempting to want to shake everything up, roll the dice, and let luck take the way. In some ways, if you're adventuresome enough and open to experimentation, you might learn as much doing this than anything I've offered here. Sure, some plants will live, and some will die. But you'll get a clear idea what works on the site and what doesn't. In a small garden, randomizing might not make a lot of sense given the rather intimate relationships of plants to one another and other features, unless you're starting from scratch and don't mind gambling a bit.

## ESTABLISHING PLANTINGS: CULTIVATING DENSITY AND SYNERGY

Constant, inevitable gardening change is practically a mantra of this book. Avoiding change is resource intense, although it's easy to find many landscapes gardened with such foolishness, restrained to some vision of creation instead of celebrated for what they've become (or could become). Plants grow. This is perhaps both our greatest hope (please, *grow*) and our most earnest plea (please, don't *grow* out of my control).

In the early years of establishing a planting, strive to cultivate dense arrangements of the plants you want and promote synergy among them whenever possible. You'll always have problem spots where plantings just never work out, but you shouldn't dwell on these. Like the coach of a major league team, invest in your top performers and build upon their success. Dutch artist and landscape architect Louis le Roy wrote, ". . . for anyone who thinks and works ecologically, the most important aspect is the management of energy." By fostering positive ecological interactions among plants and in concert with the site, a gardener in the New

Naturalism tradition conserves energy for the greatest return on investment without constant inputs. This is smarter gardening, not harder gardening.

## Preparing for Planting

Preparing the site for planting should follow your site analysis. Understanding the point from where you start makes all the difference in determining how you'll get to where you want to go. Further, the same rote, paradigmatic techniques for preparing planting beds often produce wildly different results each time they're executed. This isn't the result of poor technique; it's a mismatch between technique and site. Put another way, you wouldn't bake a chocolate cake using a recipe for chocolate chip cookies, even though they both have chocolate. Our approach to creating plantings should borrow this common-sense wisdom from the kitchen: right recipe, right result.

That being said, the archetypal recipe for site preparation requires the most unpacking from traditional methods. While there is a tendency to want to juice up soil fertility to get plants off to a robust start, this method will often backfire because of the indiscriminate nature of fertility—everything grows, including all the things you don't want such as weeds and plants with a strong tendency to compete. While it's true that a healthy humus layer is a fantastic water and carbon management tool, not all landscapes function ecologically with one. Context matters: if you garden along a woodland edge, dial up the organic matter to support the development of humus in the soil (think of it like a polymer that holds it all together). If you garden in a desert, ignore humus. Additionally, humus and soil organic matter are easily confused, and other books do a fine job of breaking down the nuances of these layers that interact and influence the growth and development of plants. My best advice is to use soil organic matter as a tool; just don't bring a sledgehammer to a job that only requires a rubber mallet.

Tillage is another oft-debated subject of site preparation. While deeply tilled sites facilitate easier planting, the disturbance induced to the soil horizons can often

Generous spacing and poor consideration for the matrix led to this herbaceous planting looking barren the year following its establishment. These conditions won't simply resolve themselves with time even as the existing plants grow. In this scenario, weeds will realize the gap opportunities faster than the plants will establish, leading to lopsided management requirements. Better planting schemes that fill the gaps with more diversity can serve as green mulch and avoid this scenario.

lead to compaction as soil particles are reaggregated under the tread of human feet and equipment. It also disturbs existing, complex networks of microbes, the friendly cohorts that naturally foster healthy vegetation. Further, tilling the soil even a few inches deep releases carbon into the atmosphere as soil aggregates disintegrate, and tilling increases the likelihood of runoff and erosion. Extensive research in sustainable agriculture supports the idea of keeping soil organic carbon in place to promote higher biological activity and a more resilient environment in the face of drought. Tilling disrupts all of this.

Disturbance from tillage and planting introduces new weed seed to the surface where they readily germinate; a few inches of mulch can greatly reduce weed pressures during the first year of the establishment. The type of mulch depends on the context and climate too. In an open, sunny, and otherwise productive situation, organic mulches such as finely shredded hardwood or coarse, composted leaves would do the trick. In a stressful, dry setting, inorganic mulches of gravel and fine stone fit the look and the reality that most plants adapted to those circumstances thrive in lean conditions. Ideally, for the greatest resonance with place, the type of mulch you select should have some relationship to the site; pine needles for former pine barrens or shredded leaves for woodlands and woodland edges, for example. First, it's sensical—use what's available. Second, it minimizes introducing more biochemical variables to the site. Knowing something about your site will help you navigate choices for mulches and soil amendments, if necessary. If you do mulch, be sure it's not contaminated with weed seeds if at all possible. A reputable supplier should be able to tell you how the mulch was stored in their yard.

To prepare for planting, it never hurts to inventory the existing weeds on the site. These real-time clues foretell challenges you could face in the early days of establishing the planting. Sometimes these are weeds of the garden past. Sometimes they are persnickety annual weeds lurking in the seedbank waiting for tillage to reawaken them. Paying attention to the composition of existing weed communities can give you a clue as to when to establish the planting. If you're battling weeds that germinate in warm, wet conditions such as those found in midcontinental summers, consider installing the new planting as early in the growing season as possible so that the plants you actually want have a head start on those that you don't. Similarly, instead of waiting for the perfect moment to plant, ensure that there's a redundant level of abundance within any particular layer of your plan, to provide as many chances of outcompeting any existing site pressures. However you choose to prepare the planting, keep an eye on the existing conditions of the site. The most recent stable state of the site looms large on the near-term future barring some kind of nuclear reset.

## The Act of Planting

Cultivating the density required for success starts at the time of planting. After all your planning, the real test of your ideas in concert with site begins when you dig the first hole. But at the point you're ready to commit shovel to ground with plants sitting in rows waiting for their new homes, you need to get comfortable with the

## What Are You Planting?

You have a list of plants, but what are you actually planting? Larger, containerized perennials? Bare-root trees and shrubs? What about plants grown as plugs or liners, the sort of product that commercial nurseries use to grow the larger plants you typically buy at retail? Across the world, there's a quiet shift afoot to more sustainable production systems that consume less peat and plastic, two of horticulture's biggest sins, and yield smaller plants that establish quite readily. For many gardeners, this reality is still forthcoming. Regardless of the sizes of plants to which you have access, consider this: smaller plants with good root systems actually establish faster than larger plants with extensive root systems that often suffer from greater physiological stress post-transplanting. Certainly there are exceptions, particularly for plants that don't transplant easily at small sizes or when you might need instant gratification by using larger plants at the outset. All told, the future is smaller and more economical or, at least, with a better value proposition: gardeners get more plants for their money.

A 4- to 5-inch (10-to 12.7-cm) deep plug.

idea that planting communities challenge nearly every notion of spacing that's held up righteously as prudent horticulture. You've done the math and calculated the spacings. It's likely with a lot of plants spaced so often that you'll find it isn't enough.

It's good to be dense. Density promotes competitive interactions between plants of similar and different kinds, which has the effect of self-thinning over time—weaker individuals will succumb to the stronger ones, which exert a suppressing influence on plants around them. In the case of mitigating weeds, this is a good thing. You should also consider that not all plants are equal aesthetically or ecologically. Some species suffer when planted at density from diseases such as mildews on account of poor airflow and circulation. In this case, without a rap sheet for every plant in the garden, let experience in your garden be your guide. Always defer to your insights and understanding of plants, their life histories and habits, and how they proliferate.

If you're starting from scratch, laying out a new planting can be both exhilarating and mind-warping. Where did all these plants come from? Every project is different and gardeners differ in how to approach the planting process. If it's a large area, you likely already know the dimensions, so making a grid system could be logical and convenient. At the point you start putting plants on the ground, I often find it's easiest to start with structural plants first if you have them in your design. I work slowly and methodically from the largest plants in the fewest quantities to the smallest plants in the largest quantities, following the layered typology through to the end. If you plant the matrix last, you'll practically force yourself to find a way to cram all those little plants into every nook, cranny, and gap. I try to pay hyper-close attention to the quality of the plant groupings at the edges. A planting is often judged by its edges, which also receive the most disturbance of any area of the planting. Getting this right ensures a planting of greater integrity.

I also prefer to lay out one species at a time, occasionally laying out small groupings if they're vital to the essence of the planting or something I want to get right as a keystone for the rest of the process. While it can get difficult toward the end to juggle all the implications in your mind, if you're hedging your bets on your seminal, durable assumptions, it's likely to work out more often than not. However artificial the comparison, this idea of thinking one species at a time is in line with how nature operates; for all the associative inferences made from plants in communities, plants exist as individuals across the gradient of the environment.

When laying out a planting, spacing can become a visual estimation that lacks precision. But at the point just before plants go in the ground, it's easy to make minor adjustments if something doesn't quite look right to your eye. Just take care not to make any gaps bigger than they already are. Our native tendency is to want to give each plant a comfortable ring of air in which it can breathe. It looks tidier that way too. Density, however, is our friend.

Take a deep breath; this is supposed to be fun. Remember, this is only the beginning. Most things will persist; a few won't. See these challenges as opportunities to just keep planting. While there is often a trade-off with disturbance, the act of planting over time helps diversify the structure of populations of any given plant in your garden. Especially given an understanding of longevity, periodic replanting of certain spaces may be necessary to ensure they persist.

## After Planting

Deciding how to establish your new planting and with what also has ecological trade-offs beyond personal economics and feasibility. One theory from the scientific literature relates to the density and compositions of new plantings at the outset: plant communities assemble through selection of the colonists, the initial species that occupy niches post-disturbance. You can think of plants in a new garden like newcomers to an uninhabited island. Absent anyone else telling them what to do, the newcomers make the rules, use the resources available for their own interests, and succeed as a result of their ability to establish in this new order and reproduce. This rule also applies to the stowaways, the unseen seedbank present in any site that can quickly assert its presence in the early days. What these weeds are matters, of course. Some early weeds aren't long-term problems. But lurking beneath a freshly killed plot of turf or a lightly raked planting bed are the propagules of the remnant stable state, often both annual and perennial species keen to reestablish in the niches available to them in the new order. Here you're a gardener turned adjudicator. As the referee, you have to call the shots from the very beginning in favor of the plants you ultimately want to dominate the site.

In the early years of establishing a new planting, the weeds you'll battle are the equivalent of the old guard, usually already well established in the seed-bank and happy to rear their heads in reaction to your efforts. These were likely present when you did an initial survey of the weeds and vegetation on your site. The goal with weeding in the early years is to tip the balance in favor of the things you've planted by reducing competition from weeds. Seems simple enough, right? Except the best way to do this is to invade as minimally as possible, focusing first on removing perennial weeds and preventing annual weeds from going to seed. Most gardeners have had at least one experience where weeding seems like Sisyphus and the stone—once you've finished a row of weeding, you have to begin again. The culprits are annual weeds, the likes of which can complete multiple generations in a single growing season, each one initiated by some level of disturbance in response to a gap in the planting. By promoting an initial competition in favor of the species you've planted, you'll eventually create a dense, competitive garden that can resist invasion from weed species.

It's worth keeping in mind, too, that microscale disturbances occur in gardens all the time. Even digging a hole a season or two after planting counts as disturbance, if on a small scale. Remember that disturbance and any resulting stress is part of nature's way of keeping things interesting. A little disturbance in the garden usually doesn't hurt, so long as a little doesn't quickly become a lot, which can lead to a revolt of the previous landscape condition (like a weedy,

This spring season gap, not unlike those in many traditional gardens, results from an incomplete guild of compatible species. By late summer, there's no trace of it as the large *Molinia* 'Cordoba' (Cordoba moorgrass) assume their full size at the height of the growing season. But in the early days of spring, there's not a ground layer to occupy that space, which leads to increased weeding and management. The key to filling this gap is finding species that complete most of their life cycle in spring so that they don't suffer in the shade of the *Molinia* later.

compacted lawn) and reintroduce nuisance weeds into the planting.

In 1977, ecologist Peter Grubb published the concept of the regeneration niche, which posits that a plant species cannot persist if the conditions of the site only promote the growth and development of adults. Put another way, if a site doesn't allow the reproduction and the success of seedlings, a species won't persist. In the garden, this happens often, especially given the prevalence of sterile cultivars or plants that don't readily produce seeds because humans have intended it that way. Recent research has extended this idea to pollination activity; in order to produce seeds, there has to be successful transfer of genes between plants in the first place. If plants aren't getting it on with the bees while they're flowering, they may not be the best choices for long-term resilience.

### Encourage self-sowing and consider establishing plantings from seed at larger scales

While most of this book deals with the establishment of garden schemes from plants, seed provides a cost-effective means for growing biodiverse gardens,

(LEFT) Once it's established, you'll never be without the Brazilian roadside annual *Verbena bonariensis* (purpletop). Absent competition, it can form voluminous stands as shown here in conjunction with *Gaura* Star Struck™, a dynamic duo that filled voids in this planting for the first season as other perennials and shrubs established. Inexpensive, effective, and beautiful—who cares if it's not permanent?

(ABOVE) Ruderal plants will frequently manipulate opportunities within a planting and occur wherever they can gain a foothold. That sense of serendipity is magical and can lead to little wayside communities of reseeders such as *Talinum paniculatum* 'Limon' (Jewels of Opar) and *Eschscholzia californica* (California poppy).

(TOP RIGHT) Years ago I acquired seed of the wild-type, night-flowering, Brazilian native *Nicotiana alata* (flowering tobacco) from Canadian seedswoman Kristl Walek. It's become a staple in my repertoire of reseeding annuals, a joyful jester that plays to adoring crowds alongside a cast of summer favorites. Where there's a gap, there's a stand of *Nicotiana alata* and almost always, there are hummingbirds and sphinx moths.

(BOTTOM RIGHT) Seed from suppliers of native species is often a wonderful trove of genetic diversity, but plant it densely. Not only will the best individuals survive, most seeds won't ever manage to germinate; it's a simple law of nature. Unlike a cultivar with a reasonable degree of performance expectations, an array of genotypes within a seed mix will expectedly perform differently.

particularly when considered at a larger scale. While establishing plant communities from seed can require a few years' commitment to see through to a legible result, crafting plantings as a combination of plants and seed can yield advantages for budget-conscious gardeners who also want some amount of instant gratification. First, overseeding freshly planted gardens with a simple mix of one or a few ruderal, short-lived species can close gaps in the planting and minimize weeding in the first season. It can also complicate weeding if you can't readily discern the difference between what you've sown and the weeds. Second, seeding can help to shore up plantings that might have trouble establishing. Sometimes environmental pressures (such as heavy clay or sandy soil, as extreme examples) can reduce the likelihood of transplant success and require a mix of strategies to achieve the garden you desire. In either condition, ruderal species rarely become problematic in the long run as the number of available niches declines due to competition from longer-lived, larger, and more vigorous plants. Sowing seed also ensures the highest level of functional trait diversity in the resulting population.

The trade-off of using seed in conjunction with plants is that the seeded species easily outnumber the latter, at least in the beginning. In the case of oversowing perennial plants with seeds of other perennial species, the seeding can ultimately have an outsized effect on determining what the planting will look like over time. To what degree depends on the species involved and how they interact initially. There's something fresh and wildly unpredictable about this that can be exciting on a planting of medium scale where things can develop in response to the nature of the site and where you can rein it in should it try to run off into the sunset. For those same reasons, it's probably a strategy most gardeners will avoid.

Of course, plants produce seed whether we want them to or not. Relying on plants that form persistent seedbanks has its benefits: why not invest in an insurance policy for the garden? Reseeding as a general tendency is an unsung virtue, even if some gardeners bristle at the roving tendencies of plants with a penchant for casting seed. Wouldn't you rather pull weeds of your own devising than unwanted interlopers? If weeds happen, I'm at least fine planting a few for myself. When asked what a weed is, I often parlay Ralph Waldo Emerson's adage that, "A weed is simply a plant whose virtue has not yet been discovered." We have a lot to discover.

Seedbanks also help create variable age structures and cultivate greater levels of genetic diversity in designed plant communities. Individual plants of different ages and slightly different fingerprints help create more resilient stands that can withstand disease or severe weather events. This concept is most evident using a forest analogy—if all trees were the same age, what part of the forest would be left if a storm took them all down? In a garden setting, seedbanks are most likely to come in handy where disturbance is higher, such as along a driveway or garden path and in soils with relatively low productivity. As a reminder, in soils with lower productivity, individual competitors have a more difficult time establishing to their full advantage, so gaps tend to remain present or increase throughout the lifespan of the planting. Reseeders can perennially come to occupy these gaps as long as they persist.

## BEYOND YEAR FIVE: MANAGING THE GARDEN WITH A PLAN

Traditional gardens are overly cultivated, literally and proverbially. The constant fussing, replanting, and busy activity rob the garden of its natural networks both above- and belowground. In an ecological garden, the tapestry is as important as any individual thread. The goal of gardening on the wild side, both for looks and cause, is to find some harmony between what the garden does and what you have to do with it. While achieving some desired result feels good, the real result of a wild-spirited garden is never static. Living in this kind of garden requires rethinking your approach—nothing about a garden of this sort is maintained because maintenance implies stasis. Instead, these gardens should be managed for life.

In just a few seasons, turf varieties of *Carex* (sedge), such as *C. pensylvanica*, will form continuous mats of foliage from a network of tillers just below the surface of the soil. The mounds represent the plugs that were used to establish the colony. As a lawn replacement or a monoculture groundcover in shade, these require a single annual mowing akin to the herbivory or fire that might otherwise remove their biomass in the wild. This management regime matches the ecology of the plant in place.

While this chapter places a lot of emphasis on a craftsman approach to designing initial planting schemes, you'll realize more long-term success when you plan and plant for successional change. Just like in nature, succession will ultimately influence the composition and character of a planting over time. Some plants will diminish or die altogether, and others will fill the gaps, reflecting changes in the structure of the community and the available niches. While most gardeners might grade their success based on whether a plant lives or dies, over the lifespan of naturalistic plantings, it's more important to judge success by managing to achieve an overall level of plant diversity. The goal is stability with regard to the number of different kinds of plants as opposed to the sum total of any one kind. This becomes the foundation of your planning and planting, which is as much of a philosophy as anything written or drawn.

In gardens, traditionally, succession results in a loss of diversity as a handful of plants outcompete others and take over a planting. Often the nature of plants we perceive as unruly is in response to some condition we've created or exacerbated in the garden. Many gardeners have made initial forays into naturalistic gardening only to feel overrun by plants that have simply responded to the fertile or abundant conditions of the site. While some of this may be inevitable or unpredictable, you can respond accordingly by closely monitoring plant performance and the introduction of plants over time.

At the start of each growing season, it's good to check in with the garden after its quiescence. Before blindly committing time to rote gardening activities, ask yourself what you're hoping to achieve. The point isn't just to make more work for yourself but to commit energy toward the most meaningful results while enjoying the activity. The following sections can form the mantra of gardening that starts first with observation, which then filters into activity in response to the structure of the planting, its function, and how it's changed.

### Evaluate survival and note what thrives

Often gardeners have the lowest expectations of their efforts hoping that a plant they coddled after planting will simply survive. It's important to note what survived and what didn't; even the best designs have failures. To wryly borrow verse from the late, great gardener Christopher Lloyd of Great Dixter, "The great wonder in gardening is that so many plants live." Gaps are easy enough to fill, but what with? Taking note of the plants that thrive—the ones that sailed through the winter, bounced out of dormancy, and rolled into the growing season at full speed—starts to shed light on the plants that positively respond to your site. Plant more of these. There's something deeply reassuring about this advice from Irish garden designer Helen Dillon: it's not about what you put in, but what you take away. Appending that wisdom with an ecological footnote: it's not about all the things you plant, but rather what persists. For all the supposed features and benefits we plant for, and there's surely a laundry list of these ornamental notions of leaf and flower, gardens thrive (or not) based on the performances of those decisions over time. Successful plant performances reflect the durable assumptions of the planting, even if they evolve, and the nature of the place. Even the most brilliant designers can't predict on every occasion which plants will live and which will die against the infinite forces of nature present in any landscape, which often operate on a more expansive biological scale than the relative smallness of the plant community you're cultivating. Take care not to delude yourself with any newfound illumination—the more you know about ecological gardening, the more you recognize that it's still gardening but with different rules of engagement. In fact, engagement is the point.

### Restart your garden rather than clean it up

For all the references to "cleaning up" in garden books for the last century, you'd swear gardens were dirty or sullied. While the conclusion of winter brings about a necessary period of garden work, I prefer to think of this as a restart rather than a refresh. As the garden reenters an active period, how you steward the return of life should be the focus of your efforts. If it were a mantra, restarting the garden would focus on how to cycle organic matter. The ecology of the planting will dictate how to do this, something I'll address in the following chapters alongside the planting palettes. In general, plantings based on grassland precedents usually require some kind of mowing that turns a great volume of biomass into a finely shredded mulch that pragmatically restricts weed growth and hastens its own decomposition. Woodland-inspired gardens may just need general tidying to convey care and purpose or to alleviate the suffocation of fallen leaves that can occur when tree canopies are dense. Admittedly, woodlands tend to hold most of their carbon in tree wood but cultivating a densely vegetated understory only serves to keep more of the remaining carbon locked away in the ground where it belongs. Gardens in xeric conditions or climates actually need to remain lean, so removing organic matter is often important so as not to let water accrue where it could damage the crowns of plants that prefer it dry.

Regardless of the technique or ecology, restarting the garden shouldn't be a destructive activity. If you've left most of last year's growth for the winter, you've done an enormously good deed for overwintering creatures. Try to tread gently on their homes by waiting until as late as possible before beginning to cut back or remove debris. The exact timing for invertebrates correlates with the conclusion of their winter diapause, a transition triggered by photoperiod and temperature for many species.

### Weed smarter, not harder

Weeds thrive on disturbance, a force of nature's engine. Even the most ecologically conceived gardens feature some disturbance; they are gardens, after all, not wild ecosystems. By whatever definition you choose, weeds are either adventive or voluntary. Both of these conditions challenge a gardener's need for some control. There are two problems with weeding in the way we traditionally approach it. First, it's highly subjective and often relies on your knowledge of what you planted and what you didn't, which can lead to reactively removing anything that's unfamiliar. There seemingly aren't enough good weed identification tools available in the world, but in some regions, you might find good resources through a university Extension Service, botanical garden, or conservation organization. Perhaps as a process of elimination, it's helpful to know what seedlings of desirable species look like so that self-seeding communities can begin to develop. Second, it's a highly disturbing activity, often stirring up more weed seeds from the relatively shallow pan of the seedbank resting in the crust of the soil or just below it amid other organic matter.

What kind of New Age approach to weeding am I espousing? Think of it as stewardship instead of a battle. Weeding reduces the biomass of some plants at the expense of others. But while it might be obvious that you have weeding to do, you should consider why those weeds exist in the first place. Most weed species have an opportunistic streak, so to pose it another way, what opportunity exists that allows these weeds to infiltrate? Weeds are the symptoms; opportunity is

(TOP) The composition of this planting raises a routine gardening question—should something as adept in its ability to cover area like *Lysimachia clethroides* 'Heronswood Gold' (Heronswood Gold gooseneck loosestrife) be reined in from time to time? Frame this question ecologically and horticulturally: does it reduce diversity, and does it disrupt the legibility of the design? Regardless of the plant and its origins, it is an opportunity to think beyond the art of planting toward the ecology of gardening.

(RIGHT) When it comes to plants with wild personalities, I have a rule about how to articulate and associate them with other plants: give them a recognizable partner. When you allow something such as *Anthriscus sylvestris* (cow parsley), which might rightly be considered a weed in some parts of the world, alongside *Allium stipitatum* 'Mount Everest' (Mount Everest ornamental onion), you give it permission to let loose.

the issue. Further, if you're unsure whether to weed or not (some plants that you've planted might make you wonder), ask yourself, what is the plant doing? Is it suppressing growth of plants that could be beneficial in the long term? If yes, intervene swiftly. If it's relatively innocuous and would ultimately succumb to the density of larger plants later, don't lose any sleep over it. Ultimately, you're the referee, but in calling balls and strikes, exercise good ecological jurisprudence.

Even as an intervention, weeding isn't bulldozing. When you weed, you should graze with your hands, the sort of thing that would happen without you if large herbivores were to retake the land. (If you garden near livestock, you probably have different feelings about this, but I digress.) Obviously, you want to protect your investment but take care not to inflict more disturbance than necessary to avoid exacerbating the very problem you're trying to resolve. While a clean, cultivated look entices an agrarian fantasy, try to resist the temptation to denude the ground with each weeding. Take a triage approach. Remove the most pernicious, perennial weeds first, as these competitors with taproots and rhizomes will cause the most long-term headaches. Also remove annual weeds that can contribute mightily to the seedbank and persist even under competition; these are often recurring nightmares. For cool-season annuals that are often outcompeted in later parts of the growing season, avoid removing them if that task is overwhelming. Cool-season annuals only tend to persist given inadequate competition during their peak life cycle (late winter and early spring). For other annual weeds, deadheading should do the trick. Steady, targeted weeding in this fashion, with a focus first on where the fewest and/or most challenging weeds grow, often keeps weed populations at a minimum (with the exception of especially noxious species or unique site conditions). Also, if you can, find something enjoyable about weeding. I do my best thinking when I'm down on one knee with a furrowed, discerning brow: It's inexpensive therapy too.

### Keep the planting legible

Your planting will grow and evolve with time—that's what it's supposed to do. The goal is less about preserving some perfect plant combination and more about preserving the visual essence of the garden—its overall diversity, charismatic plants, and their profiles—in the context of the landscape. Whatever happens, enjoy the ride and strive to keep the scene worth living in. Remember, clean lines and artful gestures can go a long way toward conveying intention around plantings that some might still regard as messy on the best days. The best days, by the way, are good reminders of the value of strong seasonal themes and emblematic moments. It's like the loud, vivacious part of your favorite piece of music that gets you on your feet or in the groove. The whole song isn't like that, but there's always the refrain or that one verse that makes it all come alive. Plant more of those moments or at least ensure those you already have planted get put on repeat.

### Cultivate greater diversity by keeping the garden lean

Plant communities have a way of self-regulating; when one plant dies another, often different, species replaces it. Density is self-regulating. A whole host of factors influences how this happens, from the presence of sun or shade, the size of the gap, the type of soil surface, and the pressure of herbivory. But it underscores the value of keeping the planting dense and diverse, even if mostly as a form of self-insurance.

Diversity, as you've seen, often correlates strongly with surprisingly lean, infertile circumstances. Research has demonstrated that the cost of managing a landscape increases as the organic matter of the soils increases, which smacks at conventional ideas about soil fertility. Remember, this isn't an agricultural field. By facilitating organic matter appropriately each season, you're essentially fostering a healthy soil biome that naturally feeds plants. In an ecologically functional landscape, success isn't measured by the circumference of a dinnerplate dahlia or the heft of a juicy tomato. It's measured tactically by abundance and function, and, experientially by pleasure and observation.

# PLANTING PALETTES

## A Few Words about the Palettes

Authors Richard Hansen and Friedrich Stahl wisely observed in their book *Perennials and Their Garden Habitats*, "It is always dangerous to give recipes for successful planting." I kept this wisdom close at hand as I worked on this section.

While it might seem simplistic to carve up the prototypical residential landscape into convenient districts, the ideas espoused in the following chapters aren't intended to be prescriptive as much as suggestive, a starting line for a new gardening adventure. The palettes and their components consider ecology first but, given the global readership of this book, are agnostic to the vibrancy or nuances of locality. From this conceptual foundation, I hope you'll gain confidence to follow your intuition and seek out the best plants for and of your region. Along the way, I describe common ecological parameters that you might encounter in the home landscape in hopes of inspiring your thinking wherever you garden. As you develop your own palettes, focus on establishing core guilds that you can continue to replicate and elaborate upon through additional plantings as they prove successful. Strive to plant more diversely than you have before.

With only general context, these are merely lists of plants; a single note isn't music by itself. The plants listed are generally available in the horticultural trade and are quintessential representatives of the palette concept even when they're not the most overt or common. I've endeavored to omit the standard fare when there were newer options to highlight. The supporting images come from a wide range of gardens across the globe, some wilder than others. We could always

be wilder. In consideration of the scale of most home gardens, the palettes focus heavily on herbaceous perennials and shrubs except where noted.

The palettes build on the layers introduced in the previous chapters to help you categorize plants by their functional properties, specifically where they fit into the greater planting scheme. The goal is to think about planting choices in a different way, toward a functional end, not merely an ornamental one. Functional planting choices have scalar benefits to the ecology of place. By stretching the boundaries of your existing knowledge, I hope to expand your view of what plants can do in relationship to place and one another.

The lists within each row aren't all meant to be partners as much as they are options within that category and given condition (biscuits, muffins, and bagels are all breakfast carbohydrates, but are hardly similar in taste). Context matters both horticulturally and ecologically. Every note might not be in tune with your climate, landscape, or planting approach. As I'm prone to say: too many plants, too little time. Within the vignette rows, I've tended to omit seasonally emblematic plants out of brevity.

Where utilized, the distinctions between moisture gradients are admittedly blurry on occasion. Some plants can just take it all; others are site-specific and niche oriented. Where applicable, I attempted to cross-list species that might span the gamut between the noted extremes.

In all, this narrative spans a considerable spectrum of ecological realities. Apply locally. Ask yourself, "Why should I grow this here and what will it do?"

---

Vignettes like this aren't merely a result of dense initial planting, but rather, the proliferation of many species under common conditions to fill the niches available.

# 4   OPEN LANDSCAPES

**FULL SUN.** Those two words on a plant label can be both a blessing and a curse. Without saying how many hours of sun or at what angle it drenches the landscape in its golden rays, garden advice regarding exposure tidily overestimates and generalizes the realities of planting in open spaces. Open landscapes include everything from a sunny patch of half-grown lawn to a windblown, exposed bluff overlooking the ocean.

Context is everything, even if light shines from above. In some ways, having ample exposure is unlikely in many urban settings. Only in suburban or rural areas do gardeners enjoy the blessings of unimpeded sunlight. Surely it depends on where you live and garden, but then again, the precedents simply organized by light exposure vary as widely from desert floor to alpine meadow to riverine grassland. For all the good

garden plants featured, ranging from cactus to cushion plants to *Carex*, the palettes and examples offered in this chapter aim to take advantage of openness while also preserving it.

For all the contemporary fascination with meadows, it's worth a short diatribe to put the term in context. Meadows are agricultural inventions, gently managed grasslands in the hands of humanity for centuries by crop rotation, grazing, or seasonal haying. In effect, a meadow is a garden on an agricultural scale. This is one of the inconvenient truths about the seemingly fragmented natural world of today: humans and even large megafauna before us have disturbed the landscape and its workings for thousands of years. Of course,

meadows may only be the term du jour because the idea of a prairie or full-blown grassland intimidates people. If you've ever walked in one, grasses towering over you, it's likely not the first thing that comes to mind when you imagine planting one in your home landscape. The notion is inherently romantic only if

An open, exposed hillside gravel garden at Chanticleer in Wayne, PA, USA, uses a restricted grasses palette as scaffold for a looser cohort of *Echinacea tennesseensis* 'Rocky Top Hybrids' (Tennessee purple coneflower), *Consolida regalis* (larkspur), *Nassella tenuissima* (Mexican feather grass), and assorted *Penstemon* (beardtongue). In dry conditions, promoting reseeding species keeps the garden in perpetual motion.

you don't have to consider gardening it. Meadow as parlance seems like a safe space.

Dispensing with unfounded hopes and dreams, if we plan to borrow inspirations from wild plant communities in the open, we almost automatically embrace the likelihood that these plantings will feature herbaceous plants heavily if not exclusively. Throughout the palettes and precedents offered, at nearly every scale, grasses and grasslike plants are essential for capturing the essence, whether used abundantly or precisely. Grasses almost always count members of the aster and legume families as close associates, a helpful clue for rounding out the guilds you might plant. Intermingling plants with careful thought for how light penetrates to the lowest layer of leaves can yield unexpected combinations and dreamy results. Maximizing the prevalence of flowering plants in drifts and seasonal waves while cultivating tidy and articulate edges round out the checklist of features to note.

These plantings should stretch if not snap free from the hierarchical norms of traditional planting, favoring complexity and discovery.

Despite herbaceous favoritism, there are great opportunities to use shrubs to blur the edges between the canopies and open space while also framing vignettes for herbaceous perennials to shine. The chaparral precedents of Mediterranean climates come to mind. Used to articulate and punctuate, shrubs can do service as a legible framework to tame the wildness we might flirt with. It's not just a "bunch of grass" in the pejorative sense.

If space permits, open exposures encourage plants to stretch toward the sun to dazzling architectural effect. Take this confab averaging 5 feet (1.5 m) tall: *Andropogon gerardii* 'Dancing Wind' (Dancing Wind big bluestem), *Coreopsis tripteris* 'Gold Standard' (Gold Standard tall tickseed), and *Vernonia* 'Southern Cross' (Southern Cross hybrid ironweed).

## GROUND RULES BY LAYERS

### Matrix

From a bird's-eye view, you could interpret plant communities in the open as endless and unfolding assemblages of species intermingling to form a fairly complex matrix. But at ground level, there's a working cohort that makes these systems churn, often of sedges, grasses, rushes, and cool-season perennials. In plantings, they can be visually interesting all season or fade to the background when appropriate; it's your choice. Just don't forget them entirely. It's easy to lean heavily on the later lushness of tall perennials, which form a green umbrella of vegetation over the ground, but these don't jump to life in the first two weeks of spring. They take time, and time is an opportunity for something else, potentially undesirable, to fill the void. Many famous plantings look smashing in September and boring in May for the same reason. With all the flourish saved for late in the season, the early chapters of the growing season don't have much of a plot line. Overcoming this early season bareness—what some gardeners call "the gap"—becomes a perennial, but rewarding challenge, stretching our palettes beyond the usual availability to include spring-flowering, summer-dormant ephemeral species (such as *Polemonium* or some species of *Papaver*), or spring-awakened emergents that grow and persist throughout the season such as many species of *Solidago* and *Chrysanthemum*).

### Structure

To preserve a looser, natural feeling, grasses and perennials become key to the visual architecture. In some cases, stemmy, copse-forming shrubs with transparent framework, particularly in spring and fall, have a lot of value particularly if set in the background. Trees of the thicket edge, such as *Prunus* (plums), *Amelanchier* (serviceberries), and *Salix* (willows), serve well in this role when you can hew their character and shape with a set of sharp pruners. In truth, many plants of open spaces have no affinity for the shade of woody perennials, so if utilized at all, placement is critical so that their inevitable shade doesn't result in a loss of diversity within the planting. Coarse, tall perennials can shade out underlings too; don't plant a brute next to something more benign. The canopies of these skyscrapers continue to expand throughout summer, exacerbating this effect. For all your instincts to want to grade plants by height, consider grading them by their profiles to discover more ecological arrangements and relationships.

### Vignettes

The vignettes in an open landscape are generally the reason you make a garden in the open to begin with; dreams of Instagram-worthy plant combinations easily fill our heads. This layer leads to fun, colorful, and vivacious ideas, shrugging off the darker lot of shade garden compatriots. With all that light, it's easy for so many things to grow that choreographing plantings both for their aesthetic and ecological cadences becomes important. In effect, you're aiming to plant the spatial and temporal niches to ensure beautiful, adaptive communities. Take care not to let vast wild expanses overwhelm your focus on colorful details. At scale, grasslands aren't the most interesting until you zoom in for a closer look.

If early in the season you want to have a strong spring color layer, plan for these plants to tolerate shade later in the season, just as you did in the matrix layer, as taller, emergent, and mounded perennials will overcome them. Getting this right is tricky, but it's made somewhat easier by the fact that so many spring-flowering bulbs and perennials are truly ephemeral, tucking into the ground for another year after they've flashed their colors.

The other consequence of being spoiled for choice is the need to consider how plants look before and after they flower. If you have an open mind about plants, you can start to find subtle nuances that make plantings more interesting and dynamic, skirting green forms

A matrix of *Schizachyrium scoparium* (little bluestem) glows in russet tones in early autumn as intersecting drifts of *Perovskia atriplicifolia* (Russian sage), *Liatris pycnostachya* (prairie blazing star), and *Parthenium integrifolium* (wild quinine) form novel plant communities evoking the tallgrass prairie. Planting design by Jeff Epping for Epic Systems' corporate campus in Verona, Madison, WI, USA.

of species yet-to-flower with a so-called stitch layer of annual species. Ideally, a palette of good choices should include some plants that do double duty, flowering beautifully in assorted vignettes in mid- to late summer while offering sprawling groundcover earlier in the season. Plants such as the lax, herbaceous *Clematis heracleifolia*, *C. integrifolia*, *C. recta,* and *C. fremontii* all fill niches in exposures varying from full to part sun.

Careful plant selection can result in densely layered, legible, and immersive communities that form a column of skyward vegetation over the ground. Ten species appear in this photo representing less than approximately 10 square feet (1 square meter). *Planting by the author.*

## SUNNY AND HERBACEOUS

When designing a wild, grassy planting of perennials, you'll probably consider the diversity of textures and shapes in your composition more than any rules about heights and how they relate to one another. In one sense, meadows and prairies often feature many tall plants, so focusing chiefly on height seems to miss the magic of bringing together plants with wilder personalities for an immersive experience. Of course, on an annual basis, usually in late winter or early spring, all of that biomass that you waded through the previous season has to come down, trimmed, and mulched to aid its return to the ground as decomposed organic matter. Doing this early enough ensures rejuvenation ahead of warming soil temperatures and increasing daylength.

There is some imprecise guideline about the ratio of different kinds of plants to use in the matrix layer versus those in the taller layers of the planting. While many of the prescriptions tossed around lack substantial empirical support, it seems that the more that plant diversity increases in the upward layers for the benefit of structure and aesthetics, the less diversity is required in the matrix. While only a few species do the work, they still need to be applied at considerable numbers to get the job done. In instances where less diversity is used in the upper layers, more gap opportunities exist in the ground plane, often resulting in a visually flat scheme with only occasional taller punctuations. In order to keep things interesting, the burden of aesthetics then falls to a higher level of diversity in the matrix. Bottom line—beware of keeping things too simple. Diversity is a good thing.

In small gardens, fine-scaled textures invite close inspection and fit the frame. In larger spaces, they disappear entirely, unless exaggerated into a mass or cloud. Taking this further, diaphanous grasses (think *Panicum* (switchgrass) or *Deschampsia* (tufted hair grass)) and perennials with cumulus-like flower displays (such as *Thalictrum* (meadow rue) or *Gypsophila* (baby's breath)) embody this principle in their architecture, making for dramatic intercessions among less emphatic plant shapes.

# Planting Palette for Sunny and Mesic Conditions

Plants listed here thrive in sunny, moist, and generally fertile conditions. Consider the scale of the planting area when making choices as the stature and spread of some could overwhelm a small space. Plants marked with a (*) are often generously proportioned either in their height and/or spread to the extent that they might negatively influence plant diversity if used plentifully or densely.

Flowering at nearly 5 feet (1.5 m) tall in late summer, a mass of *Helenium* 'Flammenspiel' (Dancing Flame sneezeweed) towers well over its neighbors much as the species might in its native wetland habitat.

| LAYER | PLANTS |
|---|---|
| **MATRIX**<br>Grasses or low-growing herbaceous perennials with cool-season tendencies. Disperse throughout planting scheme as patchy colonies of many individuals to knit together guilds formed by structural and vignette plants. | *Andropogon gerardii* and cultivars (*)<br>*Andropogon glomeratus*<br>*Calamagrostis brachytricha* (*)<br>*Carex albicans, bicknellii, brevior*<br>*Packera* spp.<br>*Sisyrinchium angustifolium*<br>*Sporobolus heterolepis*<br>*Tradescantia bracteata, virginiana* (*) |
| **STRUCTURE**<br>Architectural herbaceous perennials with coarse, upright habits and varying degrees of visual rigidity. Preference shown here for tall, leafless stems that foster light penetration to lower levels of the planting. Intersperse sporadically throughout the planting in small groupings (3–7 per species) scaled to the total proportion of the planting space. | *Amsonia tabernaemontana, illustris* (*)<br>*Baptisia* spp. and hybrids (*)<br>*Ceanothus americanus, herbaceous*<br>*Cephalaria gigantea* (*)<br>*Datisca cannabina* (*)<br>*Napaea dioica* (*)<br>*Senna marilandica* (*)<br>*Silphium laciniatum, terebinthinaceum* (*) |
| **VIGNETTES**<br>Plants with definitive seasonal interest. While a variety of plant architectures are displayed here, most tolerate or withstand modest levels of competition between other garden species, but placement is important to ensure good fitness between the niche and an individual plant's profile. | *Agastache foeniculum, nepetoides* and hybrids<br>*Allium lusitanicum* 'Summer Beauty'<br>*Arnoglossum atriplicifolium*<br>*Asclepias incarnata, purpurascens, tuberosa*<br>*Boltonia asteroides*<br>*Echinacea pallida, purpurea* and hybrids<br>*Euthamia caroliniana* (*)<br>*Gladiolus communis*<br>*Helenium autumnale* and cultivars (*)<br>*Helianthus salicifolius* (*)<br>*Heliopsis helianthoides* var. *scabra* 'Bleeding Hearts' and 'Burning Hearts'<br>*Liatris pycnostachya* (*)<br>*Lilium* spp. and cultivars<br>*Macleaya cordata*(*)<br>*Monarda bradburiana, didyma, fistulosa* and cultivars (*)<br>*Ornithogalum magnum*<br>*Salvia azurea*<br>*Salvia nutans, pratensis*<br>*Sanguisorba officinalis, tenuifolia,* and cultivars<br>*Solidago rigida, speciosa, virgaurea*<br>*Penstemon digitalis, hirsutus*<br>*Physostegia virginiana* (*)<br>*Pycnanthemum flexuosum, muticum* (*), *tenuifolium*<br>*Ratibida pinnata* (*)<br>*Rheum* spp.<br>*Rudbeckia maxima, subtomentosa*<br>*Symphyotrichum novae-angliae* and cultivars<br>*Symphyotrichum oblongifolium* and cultivars<br>*Thalictrum* spp. and cultivars<br>*Vernonia baldwinii* (*), *noveboracensis* (*)<br>*Veronicastrum virginicum* (*)<br>*Zizia aurea* |

(TOP) As you make planting decisions, study the dynamic lifespans of plants on your list. Some plants such as *Agastache foeniculum* 'Blue Fortune,' a fertile hybrid selection, live for only a few seasons on loamy, fertile soils but reseed sporadically and with subtle variations in the seedlings.

(RIGHT) *Arnoglossum atriplicifolium* (pale Indian plantain) spends life as a tall, leafy emergent perennial in prairies, but has yet to catch on with most gardeners. Its ornamental rap sheet reads like personals ad for plant lovers: glaucous foliage, red-blushed stems, and patina-tinted blooms that glow in late summer light.

In this meadow-inspired front yard border, tall herbaceous perennials such as *Persicaria polymorpha* (fleeceflower) and *Veronicastrum virginicum* 'Fascination' (Culver's root) join a matrix of architectural grasses to create a dense, full vignette in late summer. Ecologically, this planting succeeds because these plants occupy large niches, leaving space for emergent emblems such as *Lilium leichtlinii* (citronella lily). *Planting by Austin Eischeid.*

## Clumping Grasses for Meadow and Mixed Plantings

With grasses now front and center, it's hard to distill such a wide berth of global plant diversity into a single list for style and function. This collection only begins to scratch the surface of recent or still unsung releases in grasses for place-driven plantings. Many warm-season grasses proliferate both vegetatively and via seed, traits that influenced the composition of this list for home gardens in favor of more mild-mannered species and selections. All species and cultivars noted here generally surpass 2 feet (0.6 m) in height.

At the dry edge of a meadow planting, matrix grasses *Schizachyrium scoparium* 'Jazz' (Jazz little bluestem) and *Sporobolus heterolepis* (prairie dropseed) infiltrate the woody, ground-covering *Salix repens* 'Bridal Rice' (Bridal Rice creeping willow). This simple vignette features three seasons of ornamental interest.

| PLANT NAME | GEOGRAPHIC ORIGIN OF SPECIES |
|---|---|
| *Achnatherum calamagrostis* Undaunted™ | Europe |
| *Andropogon gerardii* 'Dancing Wind' | North America |
| *Andropogon gerardii* Windwalker® | North America |
| *Bouteloua curtipendula* 'Trailway' | North America |
| *Bouteloua gracilis* 'Blonde Ambition' | North America |
| *Melica ciliata* | Europe and Asia |
| *Miscanthus nepalensis* | Asia |
| *Molinia* 'Dutch Dreamer' | Europe |
| *Molinia* 'Heidebraut' | Europe |
| *Muhlenbergia reverchonii* Undaunted™ | South Central North America |
| *Panicum virgatum* 'Bad Hair Day' | North America |
| *Panicum virgatum* 'Cheyenne Sky' | North America |
| *Panicum virgatum* 'Purple Tears' | North America |
| *Pennisetum* Etouffee Series | Europe and Asia |
| *Schizachyrium scoparium* 'Standing Ovation' | North America |
| *Schizachyrium scoparium* 'Twilight Zone' | North America |
| *Sesleria* 'Greenlee's Hybrid' | Europe |
| *Sorghastrum nutans* 'Thin Man' | Cultivated (North America) |
| *Spodiopogon sibiricus* | Asia |
| *Sporobolus airoides* | Western North America |
| *Sporobolus heterolepis* | Central North America |
| *Stipa barbata* | Europe |
| *Stipa gigantea* | Southern Europe |

*Melica ciliata* (hairy melic grass) is a striking cool-season bunchgrass native throughout Europe, Asia, and northern Africa, thriving in gravelly soils. It's shown here forming a matrix with romping bands of *Lychnis coronaria* (rose campion) and *L. chalcedonica* (Maltese cross). Notice the bunchy patchwork across the ground as an assembly rule defined by clumps and basal rosettes.

## STEPPE UP

In the last decade, gravel gardens have emerged as a horticultural form of the steppe with surprising versatility in varied climates. Many plants adapted to the grassy, semi-arid, continental regions of the world known as "steppes" thrive through cold, dim winters and low summer rainfall. Artificially replicating these conditions might still have a whiff of horticultural exploration; we naturally want what we can't have. If you live or garden in these regions, adopting your local system only makes good sense. But for all this fascination with granite chips and pea gravel, the movement of interest has revealed that most regions of the world contain some local precedent where lean soils and other forms of environmental stress define a uniquely suited palette of plants. Given the relatively vast areas of the world that experience these climatic patterns, examples of these palettes could run on for pages into a separate book. As with any region or ecological precedent, let plants light the way. Even if you don't set out to replicate the rugged character of the scrubby chaparral or the shortgrass plains with exacting precision, the charismatic flora of these ecosystems offer specific features worth accounting for. These rugged and sometimes demure grasses offer invaluable support for overwintering invertebrates, which while away the winter burrowed into their crowns. The seeds support both ground-dwelling birds, songbirds, and small mammals. In short, the steppes of the world harbor beloved and beneficial garden perennials such as *Perovskia atriplicifolia* (Russian sage) in Central Asia; *Sphaeralcea* spp. (globe mallows) in Western North America; and *Delosperma* spp. (ice plants) in South Africa, shining a runway light on the ecosystem as a model for stylish, resilient gardening.

In a steppe-inspired garden, minimalism is in vogue, at least ecologically speaking. When creating these systems in gardens, you have to mitigate the accumulation of organic matter (nutrients) that will accrue at the surface in order for many of these species to thrive. Many plants from these stress-prevalent regions feature conservative growth habitats for the purpose of accruing starch reserves and generally thrive with limited water and fertility. In some ways, using the layered approach, any planted matrix is supplemented by stress for the greater resilience of the plant community. Many of the grasses and grasslike plants utilized in these designs have as much structural interest, which imparts some functional value, as any ecosystem function their blades generate while covering the ground. In other words, designing stress and resource conservation into the planting scheme make for better odds of supporting plant diversity over the lifespan of the garden.

(LEFT) This rooftop planting in downtown London at the Barbican, a classic example of the concrete burdens of Brutalist architecture, grew from steppe-inspired ecology, a perfect precedent for the harsh reality of urban landscapes. In this view about a dozen species populate a 150-square-foot (14-square-meter) section. Planting design by Nigel Dunnett.

(OPPOSITE PAGE) This planting is built on a strong foundation of local natives and cultivars blended with international plants from similar habitats. *Cotinus coggygria* (smoketree) provides a bold backdrop for this assorted community including *Coreopsis lanceolata* (lance-leaved tickseed), *Penstemon digitalis* (beardtongue), *Asclepias tuberosa* (butterfly weed), and *Dianthus carthusianorum* (Carthusian pink) spackled throughout. Planting design by Jeff Epping.

## Planting Palette for Sunny and Dry Meadows

Plants listed here thrive in scree conditions with infertile, sharply drained soils, and sunny exposures. While some selections have brief bloom seasons, those listed here generally have enduring horticultural and ecological value throughout the majority of the growing season.

At nearly 5 feet (1.5 m) tall in flower, *Salvia ringens* adds depth and dimension on account of its nearly leafless stems that arise from a basal rosette. Planting by Mike Kintgen.

| LAYER | PLANTS | |
|---|---|---|
| **MATRIX**<br>Grasses or low-growing herbaceous perennials with cool-season tendencies. Disperse throughout planting schemes as patchy colonies of many individuals to knit together guilds formed by structural and vignette plants. | *Andropogon hallii*<br>*Bouteloua gracilis, hirsuta*<br>*Carex divulsa, eburnea*<br>*Delosperma* spp. and hybrids<br>*Eragrostis spectabilis, trichodes*<br>*Festuca amethystina, arizonica,*<br>    *idahoensis* 'Siskiyou Blue' | *Hesperostipa comata,*<br>    *neomexicana, spartea*<br>*Koeleria glauca*<br>*Nassella tenuissima, viridula*<br>*Schizachyrium scoparium*<br>*Sporobolus heterolepis*<br>*Stipa barbata, capillata, pennata* |
| **STRUCTURE**<br>Architectural herbaceous perennials with varying shapes, particularly tall, leafless stems that foster light penetration to lower levels of the planting. Intersperse sporadically throughout the planting in small groupings (3–7 per species) scaled to the total proportion of the planting space. | *Acanthus spinosus*<br>*Amorpha canescens, nana*<br>*Artemisia* spp.<br>*Crambe cordifolia, maritima*<br>*Cylindropuntia* spp.<br>*Ephedra minima*<br>*Eryngium yuccifolium*<br>*Kniphofia* spp. and cultivars | *Lavandula* spp. and cultivars<br>*Leucophyllum frutescens*<br>*Mahonia fremontii*<br>*Opuntia* spp.<br>*Phlomis fruticosa, tuberosa*<br>*Santolina* spp.<br>*Verbascum* spp. and cultivars<br>*Yucca filamentosa, glauca, nana* |
| **VIGNETTES**<br>Plants with definitive seasonal interest. While a variety of plant architectures are displayed here, most tolerate or withstand modest levels of competition between other garden species, but placement is important to ensure good fit between the niche and an individual plant's profile. | *Allium flavum, pulchellum,*<br>    *schoenoprasum, stipitatum*<br>*Asclepias speciosa, stenophylla,*<br>    *tuberosa, verticillata, viridis*<br>*Aster amellus* and cultivars<br>*Callirhoe digitata, involucrata*<br>*Campanula rotundifolia*<br>*Coreopsis palmata*<br>*Dianthus carthusianorum*<br>*Echinacea pallida, paradoxa*<br>*Eryngium* spp.<br>*Euphorbia corollata*<br>*Gladiolus communis*<br>*Heterotheca villosa* | *Ionactis linariifolia*<br>*Iris pumila, lactea, ruthenica, spuria*<br>*Liatris microcephala, punctata*<br>*Limonium* spp.<br>*Linum perenne*<br>*Mentzelia* spp.<br>*Monarda bradburiana, luteola*<br>*Oenothera macrocarpa*<br>*Penstemon grandiflorus*<br>*Salvia arizonica, hians, reptans,*<br>    *virgata*<br>*Symphyotrichum laeve, oolentangiense,*<br>    *turbinellum*<br>*Thermopsis lanceolata* |

(TOP) This gravel garden marries resilient plants from glades, seashores, dry prairies, and meadows to form a self-perpetuating community of plants on an exposed hillside. Planting design by the author.

(RIGHT) *Echinacea paradoxa* (yellow coneflower).

## Sunny Spackle

Every garden needs a few weeds, if you'd even call them that, that are able to close gaps quickly and effectively, a little grout between the tiles. Because of their ecological profiles, these species intercalate communities, becoming enmeshed in the characters of other plants for heightened serendipity. Utilizing plants in this way leads to unpredictable and surprising concoctions, perhaps the purest and simplest way to impart a sense of wildness regardless of your specific planting style. I've included their life history as a guide. Some species might become too weedy in some climates, so pay attention to their origins. You might discover your own style using species that already have this tendency in your garden by encouraging their proliferation.

| PLANT NAME | LIFE HISTORY | ORIGIN |
| --- | --- | --- |
| *Agalinis* spp. | Annual | Americas |
| *Allium* spp. | Annual and perennial | Cosmopolitan |
| *Anagallis arvensis* | Annual | Europe |
| *Bidens* spp. | Annual | Cosmopolitan |
| *Cleome* spp. | Annual and perennial | Cosmopolitan |
| *Consolida regalis* | Annual | Europe and Asia |
| *Cosmos* spp. | Annual and perennial | Americas |
| *Croton capitatus, texensis* | Annual | North America |
| *Eryngium* spp. and cultivars | Annual, biennial, perennial | Cosmopolitan |
| *Eschscholzia californica* | Annual | Western North America |
| *Gaura (Oenothera)* spp. and cultivars | Annual, biennial, perennial | Americas |
| *Glaucium* spp. | Annual, biennial, perennial | Europe, Africa, Asia |
| *Helenium amarum* | Annual | North America |
| *Hesperis matronalis* | Biennial | Europe and Asia |
| *Mirabilis* spp. | Annual and perennial | Americas |
| *Papaver somniferum* | Annual | Europe and Asia |
| *Phacelia* spp. | Annual and perennial | Americas |
| *Pilosella aurantiaca* | Perennial | Europe |
| *Plantago* 'Purple Perversion' | Perennial | Cultivated |
| *Salvia coccinea, cyanescens, greggii, lyrata, sclarea* | Annual and perennial | Cosmopolitan |
| *Thelesperma filifolium* | Annual and perennial | Central North America |
| *Verbascum* spp. | Annual, biennial, perennial | Europe and Asia |
| *Verbena bonariensis* | Annual | South America |
| *Verbesina encelioides* | Annual | Central and Western North America |
| *Viola* spp. | Annual and perennial | Cosmopolitan |

# CASE STUDY

The Roads Water-Smart Garden at Denver Botanic Gardens (Denver, CO, USA) showcases water conservation practices through xeric plantings best suited for home landscapes. This sinuous central walkway gracefully intersects grassy vignettes of *Stipa* and *Nassella* to reveal an unfolding tapestry of plant diversity: over 400 species along a narrow, 100-foot-long (30-meter-long) garden. The density of species packed into this relatively small space illustrates the abundance that's possible even in stress-prevalent regions where resources require specialized plant palettes.

*Allium caeruleum* (blue globe onion) reseeds in climates similar to its Central Asian steppe origins, taking root in gravelly soils to form serendipitous fireworks that pop up in the openings between *Nassella tenuissima* (Mexican feather grass). Planted and grown by Dan Johnson.

| LAYER | PLANTS |
|---|---|
| **MATRIX**<br>Low mounds of silvery, colorful perennials form a unique floral matrix dotted with graceful, caespitose clumps of native and regionally adapted grasses that thrive in low-water conditions. | *Achnatherum hymenoides*<br>*Callirhoe involucrata* var. *tenuissima*<br>*Festuca glauca*<br>*Nassella tenuissima*<br>*Stipa barbata*<br>*Tanacetum densum* ssp. *amani*<br>*Thymus praecox* ssp. *arcticus* 'Coccineus'<br>*Thymus pseudolanuginosus*<br>*Thymus serpyllum* 'Pink Chintz' |
| **STRUCTURE**<br>With a strong, informal hedge of *Pinus edulis* (pinyon pines) in the background, a handful of tall perennials or low shrubs splits the difference between the background and the path. The strong repetition of squirrelly, rocketing flower spikes adds a distinctly regional character. | *Amorpha nana*<br>*Dasylirion texanum*<br>*Hesperaloe parviflora*<br>*Pinus edulis*<br>*Salvia leucophylla*<br>*Verbascum bombyciferum* 'Polarsommer' (Arctic Summer) |
| **VIGNETTES**<br>The high desert region supports a veritable trove of plant diversity that rages against the harsh climate in a kaleidoscope of loud-mouthed blooms. Plants here were selected for robust ornamental features, but the result is a nearly constant array of floral resources available for the entirety of the growing season. | *Agastache* spp. and cultivars<br>*Allium aflatunense* 'Purple Sensation'<br>*Centranthus ruber* var. *coccineus*<br>*Eryngium giganteum*<br>*Salvia chamaedryoides* |

## ROSE GARDEN REDUX

Beloved in traditional horticulture as queens of the garden, roses have reigned supreme as the symbols of good gardening, if not also with a tinge of haughtiness among those who grow them. While the old garden roses of bygone gardens harken to their wild origins with romantic habits and squirrelly canes, modern roses amount to shapeless forms drenched in fanciful flowers. In what act or scene of a wilder garden do such dolled-up creatures emerge without looking comically out of place? At the intersection of traditional ornamental horticulture and plant ecology, you can grow and celebrate roses without having to dedicate a space solely and solemnly in their honor.

Traditionally, rose gardens tend to speak most to the collector's fascination with a single plant in a formal, tidy display that showcases excellence in cultivating them. This often means excluding any form of life that would sully their appearance with an endless barrage of sprays and fussing, including unappreciative humans. To the consternation of the rose grower, many invertebrates find rose leaves and petals palatable. The flowers, too, support many native bees across the wide and varying ranges of more than 300 species throughout the Northern Hemisphere. While there's surely some middle ground, reducing or eliminating herbicide and insecticide use during the peak foraging season would undoubtedly create a more teeming environment.

By embracing the structure of roses as the scaffold of the garden, the gardener can begin to create a space where these beloved plants can thrive in a more integrated fashion with greater plant diversity. Not every diva can sing, dance, *and* act, so having a well-rounded roster of garden castmates can carry the garden for months. Nearly all categories of roses, excep the stilted, bloom-centric canes of hybrid teas, fit into this paradigm shift.

| LAYER | PLANTS |
|---|---|
| **MATRIX**<br>Low-growing, shade-tolerant perennials with cool-season growth cycles and sturdy or unnoticeable autumn forms. Generally spreading, rounded mounds to fill ground space but still emerge vertically in the gaps. Additionally, a seedling matrix of reseeding annuals listed in the Vignettes section provides welcome substitutes for the weeds you don't want. | *Campanula persicifolia*<br>*Carex bromoides, flacca, humilis*<br>*Nepeta × faassenii* and cultivars, 'Florina'<br>*Pennisetum alopecuroides*<br>*Prunella vulgaris*<br>*Tanacetum vulgare* 'Isla Gold'<br>*Teucrium chamaedrys* |
| **VIGNETTES**<br>While roses hold their own for that spotlight moment, the rest of the year, the show must go on. By choosing a handful of essential perennials for peak seasonal transitions and repeating them throughout the planting, you can create a generous and unfolding display of interest. Accessorize with reseeding annuals with fine textures and free forms. | *Allium* spp. and cultivars<br>*Ammi majus, visnaga*<br>*Clematis* spp. and cultivars<br>*Cleome hassleriana, serrulata*<br>*Filipendula vulgaris*<br>*Foeniculum vulgare*<br>*Geranium phaeum, sanguineum, wallichianum*<br>*Iris* bearded hybrids<br>*Monarda* spp. and hybrids<br>*Muhlenbergia capillaris*<br>*Passiflora incarnata*<br>*Pelargonium* spp. and hybrids<br>*Phlox glaberrima, maculata*, 'Minnie Pearl'<br>*Potentilla alba, arguta, cinerea*<br>*Salvia elegans, leucantha, madrensis*<br>*Salvia nemorosa* and cultivars<br>*Sanguisorba minor, officinalis*<br>*Thalictrum aquilegifolium, dasycarpum, rochebrunianum*<br>*Verbena bonariensis* |

The leafy spreading habit of *Geranium wallichianum*, *Monarda* 'Raspberry Wine,' and *Tanacetum vulgare* 'Isla Gold' collide with the flower-laden canes of roses, a lesson in resilience: well-grown roses of a certain age lose nary a beat in the face of herbaceous competition. Planted and grown by Leslie Hunter, Greater Des Moines Botanical Garden.

(TOP LEFT) The expiring inflorescences of this (*Allium schubertii* (fireworks onion) offer a rejoinder to fading roses that outlasts them for months. Roses serve to mask the untidy foliage of the onions—a perfect partnership.

(TOP RIGHT) A well-placed umbel or fifty—in this case, the flowers of *Ammi majus*—leave onlookers held in visual suspense as the repetition of strong geometry carries the view over the top of hazy textures.

(RIGHT) In spring, alliums and roses deserve each other.

(TOP) Rose canes make the perfect organic trellis for roving vines such as *Clematis tangutica* 'Helios,' shown here in seed in late fall.

---

(LEFT) Occasionally, rose foliage looks the part, echoing the richer colors of its nearby associates *Verbena bonariensis* (purpletop) and *Foeniculum vulgare* 'Bronze' (Bronze fennel).

# 5  PLANTING CLOSE TO HOME

**MAKING A GARDEN** close to home is both practical and pleasurable. Spaces such as dooryards and foundation beds formed by the architectural echoes of the house provide a manageable canvas, an introduction to the joy of planting and a runway to projects of greater size and scale. The lines created by the house provide a strong framework within which to make plantings that can be expressive and experimental, yet more deliberate and composed than wilder plantings you might employ at the boundaries of your property or in more private spaces. Evocative planting strategies, like those featured in this chapter, provide alternatives to sterile hedging and the gentrified, minimalist greenery that typically encircles homes, while maintaining some semblance of control over the aesthetics of the space.

The ecology of landscapes around homes is no less rich due to its proximity to humanity. Admittedly, the areas around our homes, whether an acre in a suburb or a few hundred square feet in an urban core, are inherently disturbed. You can almost imagine a halo of disturbance to soil, canopy, and vegetation that encircles our living spaces, the result of which is often very unnatural with respect to the historic landscape. You can leverage this disturbance to your benefit to help keep plantings vibrant and interesting, provided it isn't so stressful that they can't establish readily in the first place. (There are plenty of tiny spaces between sidewalks and streets that would have been better off in concrete than as maddening temptations for gardeners.)

The built environment is a novel ecosystem, almost like that of a constructed forest where the architectural forms become de facto canopies to plantings underneath them. Broadly speaking, edge landscapes between forests and open areas could logically serve

Seating areas like this one blend the living space into the garden, offering a front-row seat to nature's action. Plan for space to relax and observe, even as you find intimate ways to live with the garden. Photo by James Golden.

as good precedents for planting inspirations, but the sky is the limit, figuratively and literally. With increasingly dense neighborhood development in cities, sunlight comes at a premium. Coupled with other harsh realities of the urban environment such as high soil and water pH, and elevated day- and nighttime temperatures during the peak of the growing season, modern-day residential landscapes bear little resemblance to a wholly natural precedent and instead, represent a cosmopolitan ecology that requires and invites creative planting.

## GROUND RULES BY LAYERS

### Matrix

The matrix in gardens close to home invites close inspection. In urban situations, soil texture and quality can vary dramatically. If you're converting an existing lawn to a garden area, beware what years of conventional lawncare may have done to the productivity of your soil. Friable, productive soils, the result of years of fertilizing, will favor the proliferation of colonizing plants with a high degree of sociality such as many *Carex* (sedge) or *Ophiopogon* (mondo grass), which could spell trouble for establishing and promoting higher levels of plant diversity in the short term. If you're simply looking to replace your turf with something more sustainable, you might desire these kinds of plants that can quickly fill voids with living green mulch that can always be peeled away later for a greater array of plants. If you're looking to create a diverse planting, avoid highly competitive plants that could dominate the new small garden with a blanketing monoculture in just a few seasons. Instead, favor an eclectic roster of plant shapes (see the sidebar on plant architecture in chapter 1) that will thread together to form a tight weave of vegetation inside a strong architectural frame.

Compaction is another reality of soils in urban landscapes and favors a more abbreviated roster of plants that can establish in root zones with low oxygen and poor structure. This is a common variable in landscapes associated with new construction and which is remedied with techniques such as air spading that reaggregate the soil profiles. At the surface, compacted soils favor stress-tolerant weeds such as clovers and *Taraxacum officinale* (dandelions), which can impose establishment pressures on new plantings. The average lawn is often rife with deep weed seedbanks when the integrity of turfgrass is compromised by compaction or soil fertility. As you evaluate and learn about your site, noting the quality of existing turf or vegetation can give you insights into what's at work beneath. In these stressful circumstances, plants you might normally consider aggressive may prove more mannerly or slower to colonize.

### Structure

In garden spaces closest to the house, structural plants complement the architecture of the home as accent specimens or foundation shrubs orbited by richer vignettes. Even if you intend to rely on architecture, a charismatic or evocative plant choice will help frame garden-scale details. In some architectural traditions, gardens float away from the house, giving the building room to breathe and placing the plantings as a destination to arrive at or pass through. This three-dimensional idea of the house within a garden jibes with an ecological mindset more so than a neatly trimmed skirt of plantings around a building. Wildlife may not care much either way if provided with appropriate food supplies and an opportunity to move between spaces.

Depending on how wild you want to get, you might consider a native hedge in your front yard to simply screen your garden from outsiders looking in. While not the most inclusive, it can certainly be a practical solution. Even if your front yard garden features more porous views to the extensional landscape, a well-sited small tree or large shrub grouping could give the planting an arborescent anchor and a bit of cover for wayward wildlife in the neighborhood. This structural note could also disrupt a less-than-desirable view from

Front yard gardens are the ultimate canvases to challenge the status quo, the last uncharted terrain for making bold gardens. I've replaced an expansive, yet poor stand of turfgrass on compacted soil with a robust meadow that builds soil and creates habitat instead. An interior pathway, which connects the house to the street, loosely inspired by the constellation Orion's Belt, outlines a long, narrow island in the middle of the yard surrounded by more generous beds on either side.

the home and break up the monotony of overhead power lines, shifting your attention to the loveliness below. In more open exposures, you may need very little in the way of woody plants and instead will borrow as precedent the grassland (no frame needed) or woodland clearing (frame already provided) as a template for your efforts. In these settings, herbaceous structural plants with coarse textures and emergent habits become key to creating strong visual order.

## Vignettes

Understanding, the relative nature of this typology, the detail layer of a courtyard garden or planting closer to the house could span the gamut from intricate to straightforward depending on your taste. Leveraging disturbance might mean utilizing more annual flowers closer to the home, which you can fuss over and play with from season to season while providing floral resources for pollinators with the added benefit of a windowsill view. If your house sits within shade, a floral layer could be completely absent or used as seasonal frosting to the more functional, textural, and

enduring layers. In wild woodlands, the closed nature of the canopy often limits floral flourishes to spring and leaves later-blooming characters to have a more solo role. In the sun, the palette expands dramatically with a floral peak occurring from mid- to late summer. For front yard gardens with lots of visibility, color, and any other aesthetic trait deserves amplification if only to communicate intention to your neighbors. Absent this, you could just as well do whatever you wanted, provided you were planting abundantly and in a site-resonant manner.

## NEW FRONT YARD

Nonnative turfgrasses cover nearly 40 million acres of the United States, where it's surely the most revered of any country in the modern world. Anyone who fires up the mower might rightly consider themselves a farmer, if only turf actually yielded anything. As a resource-intensive groundcover, it does modestly more service to the world than a hard alternative, which we'll cover in chapter 6. For all the land they occupy, front yards have the potential to be so much more than turf.

Front yard gardens not only are more inclusive of species diversity than turf monocultures, they invite connections with our neighbors by breaking a separatist and conformative norm. Front yard gardens can become living doormats to our home and lives, putting our creative selves into the world and inviting others to do the same. While homeowner associations and public policy limit this outreach in some areas, the tide has begun to shift in others that realize most of what we've dictated in our urban planning has little to do with science or sense and everything to do with psychology and politics.

Still, planting a front yard garden doesn't have to land you on the front page of your local newspaper complete with a citation and a fine. You can make ecological gardens by reducing the size of the lawn or eliminating it. Turf makes a fine pathway and a legible frame, a valuable aesthetic parameter within which your wilder inclinations can roam free. Using turf in geometric configurations such as circles or straight lines accomplishes these goals while also being relatively easy to maintain. Inside those lines, you can restrict or manage the height of plantings so they don't overcome the house and look too out of control. Edge communities, meadows, and even glades pose as good precedents for front yard plantings.

## Planting Palette for Front Yard Gardens

Plants listed here grow to approximately 3 feet (1 meter) tall (or less) and wide both in sunny and shady exposures on well-drained, average to fertile soils; they generally have enduring horticultural and ecological value throughout the growing season.

| LAYER | EXPOSURE | |
|---|---|---|
| | SUN TO PART SUN | PART SUN TO SHADE |
| **MATRIX** Spreading or low rounded habits, groundcovering, or gap-filling capacities. Disperse throughout planting schemes as patchy colonies of many individuals to knit together guilds formed by structural and vignette plants. Use proportionately more plants from either of the other categories; up to 50% of the total number of plants. | *Antennaria dioica, plantaginifolia* <br> *Bouteloua curtipendula, gracilis, hirsuta* <br> *Carex albicans, divulsa, humilis* <br> *Deschampsia cespitosa, flexuosa,* 'Pixie Fountain' <br> *Festuca amethystina, glauca, idahoensis* <br> *Fragaria* spp. <br> *Molinia caerulea* and cultivars <br> *Phlox subulata* and hybrids <br> *Phyla nodiflora* <br> *Schizachyrium scoparium* and cultivars <br> *Sedum kamtschaticum* var. *floriferum* 'Weihenstephaner Gold' <br> *Sesleria autumnalis, caerulea, nitida* and 'Greenlee's Hybrid' <br> *Sporobolus heterolepis* and cultivars | *Asarum canadense* <br> *Aster ageratoides* <br> *Carex bromoides, flaccosperma, rosea* <br> *Deschampsia cespitosa,* 'Pixie Fountain,' *flexuosa* <br> *Erigeron pulchellus* <br> *Eurybia divaricata, macrophylla* and 'Twilight' <br> *Geranium maculatum, macrorrhizum* <br> *Hosta clausa* <br> *Prunella vulgaris* <br> *Tiarella cordifolia* and cultivars <br> *Waldsteinia (Geum)* spp. |

| LAYER | EXPOSURE | |
|---|---|---|
| | **SUN TO PART SUN** | **PART SUN TO SHADE** |
| **STRUCTURE**<br>Dwarf or low-spreading woody plants, architectural herbaceous perennials; vertical, upright habits or visual dominants. Place to maximize individual plants or small groupings (3–7 per species) scaled to the total proportion of the planting space. | *Achillea millefolium* and cultivars<br>*Artemisia lactiflora* and cultivars<br>*Baptisia australis* var. *minor*<br>*Caryopteris* spp. and cultivars<br>*Clethra alnifolia* and cultivars<br>*Hemerocallis* spp. and cultivars<br>*Hypericum kalmianum* and cultivars<br>*Iris lactea, sibirica, spuria,* and *setosa*<br>*Prunus pumila* Jade Parade™<br>*Ribes* spp.<br>*Senna hebecarpa, marilandica* | *Actaea* spp. and cultivars<br>*Alchemilla mollis*<br>*Distylium* cultivars<br>*Dryopteris* spp.<br>*Fothergilla* spp.<br>*Juniperus horizontalis* and cultivars<br>*Mahonia* spp. and cultivars<br>*Neviusia alabamensis*<br>*Osmunda* spp.<br>*Paxistima canbyi* |
| **VIGNETTES**<br>Plants used primarily for aesthetic interest or floral resources, either evenly distributed for large thematic effects or in tight combinations with great artistic license; includes ephemerals and scattered emergents. | *Agastache* spp. and cultivars<br>*Aster amellus*<br>*Dodecatheon meadia, pulchellum*<br>*Echinacea* spp. and cultivars<br>*Filipendula vulgaris*<br>*Geum* spp. and cultivars<br>*Liatris spicata*<br>*Nepeta* spp. and cultivars<br>*Oenothera* spp. and cultivars<br>*Penstemon digitalis, smallii, strictus,* and cultivars<br>*Phlox glaberrima, maculata,* and cultivars<br>*Plantago* spp.<br>*Pulsatilla patens, vulgaris,* and cultivars<br>*Salvia nemorosa* and *pratensis*<br>*Solidago sphacelata* and 'Golden Fleece,' *virgaurea*<br>*Stachys officinalis* and cultivars<br>*Symphyotrichum* spp. and cultivars | *Anemone japonica* and cultivars<br>*Aquilegia canadensis, chrysantha, vulgaris,* and cultivars<br>*Begonia grandis* and cultivars<br>*Helleborus* spp. and cultivars<br>*Lamprocapnos* (*Dicentra*) *spectabilis*<br>*Primula sieboldii*<br>*Pulmonaria* spp. and cultivars<br>*Symphyotrichum cordifolium*<br>*Thalictrum aquilegifolium*<br>*Tricyrtis* spp. and cultivars<br>*Zizia aurea* |

My front yard meadow in four seasons: late spring, midsummer, late summer, and mid-fall. The progression of the seasons follows the phenology of key constituents in the community, namely *Penstemon* 'Pocahontas' (Pocahontas beardtongue) in late spring and fall and *Eragrostis spectabilis* (purple lovegrass) in summer into fall.

# Groundcovers for Replacing Lawn

In situations where you intend to replace traditional turfgrasses but preserve a lawnlike function, use locally adapted or native species with strongly colonizing tendencies (i.e., highly sociable plants). When possible, minimize mowing or select species that don't require it regularly to stay healthy and productive. The following plants exhibit strong colonial habits under optimum conditions and behave like turf in that they can tolerate some degree of foot traffic and semi-annual mowing (if mowing's necessary at all). Geographic origins are noted for the purposes of making functionally appropriate selections by region.

Admittedly, not all jurisdictions rank in their progress towards loosening restrictions on wilder aspects of private property. But when you can just let your yard go, limiting mowing to only a few times a year, your plot of former turf might surprise you. This so-called "flowery lawn" in Ireland includes natives such as *Ranunculus repens* (creeping buttercup) and garden escapes such as *Primula beesiana* (candelabra primrose) to form a diverse habitat for ground-dwelling and foraging invertebrates.

| PLANT NAME | GEOGRAPHIC ORIGIN |
| --- | --- |
| *Acorus gramineus* | Northeast Asia |
| *Agrostis pallens* | Northwestern North America |
| *Ajuga reptans* | Europe |
| *Calluna vulgaris* | Northern Europe, Africa, and Asia |
| *Carex pensylvanica* | Eastern and Midwestern North America |
| *Carex praegracilis* | North America |
| *Carex tumulicola* | Western North America |
| *Danthonia californica* | Western North America |
| *Danthonia spicata* | Eastern and Midwestern North America |
| *Delosperma* spp. | Southern and Eastern Africa |
| *Erigeron karvinskianus* | Mexico |
| *Juncus tenuis* | North America |
| *Liriope muscari* | Northeast Asia |
| *Mazus reptans* | Himalayas |
| *Mitchella repens* | Eastern North America |
| *Ophiopogon* spp. | Eastern and Southern Asia |
| *Salvia lyrata* | Eastern North America |
| *Sedum acre* | Europe and Northern Africa |
| *Thymus* spp. | Europe, Africa, and Asia |

A courtyard or terrace, like those designed into the footprints of condominiums and apartments, can offer rigid geometry to tame and frame looser, wilder plantings and invite nature closer for intimate inspection. I had the pleasure of designing one several years ago for a friend as she downsized from an expansive garden to approximately 150 square feet (14 square meters). Within this jewel box, we stuffed a garden rich with personality and details—24 different kinds of plants at the time of planting. But the plant diversity per square foot defies conventional logic—how can such an eclectic palette form a legible, coherent design without becoming a jumbled mess? In a small space, every plant counts as each player is a soloist with a riff to carry at one or various points of the season. The key was to stick to an underlying color palette and amplify or mute components throughout the season so that at any time a trio or quartet of plants carried most of the aesthetic responsibility. Inspired by the idea of inviting the adjacent woodland for a closer look, this stylized community of understory dwellers quickly formed a tightly woven carpet in shades of blues and greens. In a small space where disturbance, either natural or man-made, is likely high, you have two choices for managing the planting: strive for stability or roll with the punches. In the latter sense, especially on very small plots, you can adopt the motto "just keep planting" and make a personable collector's garden of kitschy plants that relate to the surrounding ecological precedent. In the former, particularly when you don't have time to fuss and putter, you need to rely on thriving, durable, and vigorous plant choices that establish quickly and thrive in a competitive, resource-rich environment.

Small spaces can still support dense and diverse palettes that form stable schemes as seen in this courtyard garden with a *Carex flacca* (blue sedge) understory. Designed by the author.

(OPPOSITE PAGE) *Tanacetum niveum* (white bouquet tansy) ties together this garden gate planting at David Culp's Brandywine Cottage, revealing its opportunism to emerge in gaps between other competitive, ground-covering species.

## Planting Palette for Courtyards with Shady Exposures

The shade-tolerant plants listed here represent functional choices for northern temperate zones across a range of soil moisture regimes with manageable tendencies in a small space, including, but not limited to, a combination of plant size, vigor, penchant for reseeding, and floriferousness.

*Lamium orvala* (balm-leave deadnettle), *Helleborus orientalis* (Lenten rose), and *Solidago flexicaulis* (zigzag goldenrod) form a structural ring that seems to keep the colonizing *Hydrophyllum virginianum* (Virginia waterleaf) in bounds, even as it effectively fills gaps in the planting. Planted and grown by the author.

| LAYER | MOISTURE | |
|---|---|---|
| | WET TO MEDIUM WET | MEDIUM DRY TO DRY |
| **MATRIX**<br>Spreading or low rounded habits, groundcovering, or gap-filling capacities. Disperse throughout planting scheme as patchy colonies of many individuals to knit together guilds formed by structural and vignette plants. Use proportionately more than plants from either of the other categories. | *Ajuga reptans*<br>*Asarum canadense, europaeum*<br>*Beesia deltophylla*<br>*Carex amphibola, plantaginea, scaposa, sprengelii*<br>*Deschampsia cespitosa*<br>*Geranium maculatum, macrorrhizum, magnificum, sanguineum,* and others<br>*Hakonechloa macra* and cultivars<br>*Hosta* spp.<br>*Hypericum calycinum*<br>*Liriope* spp. and cultivars<br>*Ophiopogon* spp. and cultivars<br>*Tiarella cordifolia*<br>*Viola* spp. | *Asarum canadense, europaeum*<br>*Carex appalachica, divulsa, woodii*<br>*Chrysogonum virginianum*<br>*Epimedium* spp. and cultivars<br>*Eurybia divaricata, macrophyllus*<br>*Heuchera longiflora, villosa*<br>*Liriope* spp. and cultivars<br>*Meehania cordata*<br>*Ophiopogon* spp. and cultivars<br>*Pulmonaria* spp. and cultivars<br>*Rubus calycinoides*<br>*Sedum ternatum*<br>*Vancouveria hexandra*<br>*Viola* spp. |
| **STRUCTURE**<br>Dwarf or low-spreading woody plants, architectural herbaceous perennials; vertical, upright habits or heightened visual dominance. Place to maximize individual plants or small groupings (3–7 per species) scaled to the total proportion of the planting space. | *Adiantum* spp.<br>*Astilbe chinensis* var. *pumila* (*A. rubra*)<br>*Calycanthus floridus* and cultivars<br>*Cephalanthus occidentalis* 'Bailoptics' (Fiber Optics)<br>*Darmera peltata*<br>*Dirca palustris*<br>*Dryopteris* spp.<br>*Hamamelis virginiana* 'Little Suzie'<br>*Ligularia dentata, przewalskii, stenocephala*<br>*Podophyllum* spp. and cultivars<br>*Polystichum* spp.<br>*Symphytum* × *uplandicum* 'Axminster Gold' | *Adiantum* spp.<br>*Bergenia cordifolia*<br>*Clematis* × *jouiniana* 'Mrs. Robert Brydon,' *heracleifolia*<br>*Collinsonia canadensis*<br>*Delphinium exaltatum*<br>*Digitalis grandiflora*<br>*Dirca palustris*<br>*Edgeworthia chyrsantha* 'Snow Cream'<br>*Helleborus* spp. and cultivars<br>*Lamium orvala*<br>*Lilium martagon*<br>*Microbiota decussata*<br>*Paxistima canbyi*<br>*Sarcococca hookeriana* var. *humilis*<br>*Viburnum cassinoides* 'SMNVCDD' (Lil' Ditty®)<br>*Zingiber mioga* and cultivars |
| **VIGNETTES**<br>Plants used primarily for aesthetic interest or floral resources, either evenly distributed for large thematic effects or in tight combinations with great artistic license; includes ephemerals and scattered emergents. | *Actaea* spp. and cultivars<br>*Anemonella thalictroides*<br>*Aquilegia canadensis, vulgaris,* and cultivars<br>*Astrantia major* and cultivars<br>*Cardamine* spp. and cultivars<br>*Disporum longistylum* 'Night Heron'<br>*Erythronium* spp.<br>*Farfugium japonicum*<br>*Phlox divaricata*<br>*Polemonium reptans, yezoense,* 'Heaven Scent'<br>*Trillium* sp. | *Aquilegia canadensis*<br>*Brunnera macrophylla* and cultivars<br>*Corydalis* spp.<br>*Erythronium* spp.<br>*Gentiana asclepiadea*<br>*Heuchera* spp. and cultivars<br>*Iris cristata, tectorum, wattii*<br>*Phlox divaricata*<br>*Scutellaria incana, serrata*<br>*Solidago flexicaulis*<br>*Spigelia marilandica*<br>*Symphyotrichum cordifolium, lateriflorum*<br>*Uvularia grandiflora* |

# CASE STUDY

In this rectangular Brooklyn, NY, USA, courtyard, a perimeter border of lush and graphic textures obscures nearby apartment buildings. The palette features a blend of urban-adapted native and nonnative plants, chosen mostly for their durability and persistence. As with many small space gardens, the palette is assorted and eclectic, but features a number of charismatic plants that create aesthetic and functional themes. (*Planted and grown by James Golden.*)

| LAYER | PLANTS |
|---|---|
| **MATRIX**<br>While there really isn't a continuous matrix of plants in this small garden, a handful of species recur throughout the schemes to create visual themes that serve a functional purpose of uniting the various vignettes. | *Carex muskingumensis*<br>*Ceratostigma plumbaginoides*<br>*Persicaria microcephala*<br>*Sedum* spp. and cultivars |
| **STRUCTURE**<br>The overall design of the garden relies heavily on architectural plants that persist visually and functionally throughout the growing season. Those heavyweights listed here are both visually dominant and shade the soil to close up gaps within the planting to create microclimates beneath them as in the case of the *Tetrapanax*. | *Cotinus coggygria* 'Velvet Cloak'<br>*Gleditsia triacanthos* var. *inermis* 'Suncole' (Sunburst™ honeylocust)<br>*Hydrangea quercifolia* 'Snowflake'<br>*Panicum virgatum* 'Dallas Blues'<br>*Tetrapanax papyrifer* |
| **VIGNETTES**<br>With an overall emphasis on foliar texture, the vignettes feature an assorted cast that lightens the mood while rounding out the community in dappled conditions. | *Aruncus aethusifolius*<br>*Foeniculum vulgare*<br>*Helleborus* spp.<br>*Ligularia przewalskii*<br>*Maianthemum racemosum*<br>*Pycnanthemum muticum* |

# Planting Palette for Courtyards with Sunny Exposures in Northern Temperate Zones

Sun-loving plants listed here represent functional choices for northern temperate zones across a range of soil moisture regimes with manageable tendencies in a small space, including but not limited to a combination of plant size, vigor, penchant for reseeding, and floriferousness.

This sunny Irish courtyard border utilizes *Aruncus aethusifolius* 'Guinea Fowl' (Guinea Fowl dwarf goatsbeard) as a matrix through the interior of the planting. *Salvia nemorosa* 'Caradonna' (Caradonna meadow sage), *Sanguisorba officinalis* 'Tanna' (Tanna burnet), and other emergents run alongside it to create a clever scheme of horizontal and vertical layers. Planted and grown by June Blake.

Strong repetitive elements in wilder plantings permit the exuberance and nuance of variation around them. *Sanguisorba* feature through the planting, including 'Pink Tanna' shown here, varying by color while offering consistent, nodding textures.

| LAYER | SOIL MOISTURE | |
| --- | --- | --- |
| | **WET TO MEDIUM WET** | **MEDIUM DRY TO DRY** |
| **MATRIX**<br>Spreading or low rounded habits, groundcovering, or gap-filling capacities. Disperse throughout planting scheme as patchy colonies of many individuals to knit together guilds formed by structural and vignette plants. | *Carex davalliana, C. flagellifera,*<br>　　*C. muskingumensis* 'Little Midge'<br>*Geranium sylvaticum*<br>*Prunella vulgaris* and cultivars | *Antennaria* spp.<br>*Arctostaphylos uva-ursi*<br>*Carex albicans, bromoides, eburnea*<br>*Erigeron pulchellus*<br>*Fragaria* spp.<br>*Geranium × cantabrigiense*<br>*Sedum* spp. and cultivars |
| **STRUCTURE**<br>Dwarf or low-spreading woody plants, architectural herbaceous perennials, including strongly caespitose grasses; vertical, upright habits. Place to maximize individual plants or small groupings (3–7 per species) scaled to the total proportion of the planting space. | *Amsonia* (dwarf cultivars)<br>*Aruncus aethusifolius*<br>*Eupatorium dubium* 'Baby Joe'<br>*Euphorbia griffithii*<br>*Gillenia trifoliata, stipulata*<br>*Hemerocallis* spp. and cultivars<br>*Iris sibirica* and cultivars<br>*Liatris spicata*<br>*Molinia* spp.<br>*Physocarpus* (dwarf cultivars)<br>*Rodgersia aesculifolia*<br>*Sabal minor*<br>*Sambucus nigra* 'Eiffel 1' (Black Tower™)<br>*Thalictrum* spp., 'Black Stockings' | *Achnatherum calamagrostis*<br>*Amorpha canescens, nana*<br>*Anthericum liliago, ramosum*<br>*Cercocarpus* spp.<br>*Diervilla* 'El Madrigal'<br>　　(Firefly™ Nightglow™)<br>*Kniphofia* spp. and cultivars<br>*Lonicera nitida* and cultivars<br>*Molinia caerulea*<br>*Ribes aureum*<br>*Schizachyrium scoparium* 'MinnBlueA'<br>　　(Blue Heaven™), 'Standing Ovation'<br>*Spiraea betulifolia* 'Tor,' 'Tor Gold<br>　　(Glow Girl®)<br>*Sporobolus heterolepis* 'Tara'<br>*Verbascum nigrum* |
| **VIGNETTES**<br>Plants used primarily for aesthetic interest or floral resources, either evenly distributed for large thematic effects or in tight combinations with great artistic license; includes ephemerals and scattered emergents. The abbreviated list for the wetter end of the moisture regime underscores that often sunny, wet environments tend to favor taller, competitive forbs, which may prove ill-suited for small space conditions. | *Asclepias incarnata*<br>*Coreopsis rosea*<br>*Dodecatheon* spp.<br>*Eryngium yuccifolium* 'Prairie Moon'<br>*Gentiana andrewsii, asclepiadea*<br>*Helenium autumnale* and cultivars<br>*Lobelia cardinalis, siphilitica*<br>*Primula* spp.<br>*Rudbeckia subtomentosa* 'Little Henry'<br>*Salvia pratensis*<br>*Sanguisorba officinalis* 'Tana'<br>*Silene flos-cuculi* | *Anthericum ramosum*<br>*Asclepias tuberosa*<br>*Aster amellus, dumosus*<br>*Coreopsis verticillata* and cultivars<br>*Dianthus carthusianorum*<br>*Echinacea* spp. and cultivars<br>*Eryngium campestre, planum, yuccifolium*<br>　　'Prairie Moon'<br>*Euphorbia polychroma*<br>*Galatella sedifolia*<br>*Hylotelephium* spp. and cultivars<br>*Oenothera missouriensis*<br>*Rudbeckia fulgida* var. *deamii* and cultivars<br>*Salvia nemorosa*<br>*Scutellaria baicalensis*<br>*Solidago odora*, 'Dansolitlem' (Little<br>　　Lemon™), 'Loysder Crown'<br>*Tradescantia bracteata, tharpii*<br>*Verbascum nigrum* |

Weeds in pots or pots full of weeds? On a quick scan of plants in my nursery, I discovered a situation of trading places: plants I wanted with stowaways and stowaways I admired. I threw together this container one spring with these eclectic ingredients to celebrate the ephemerality of reseeding *Aquilegia* (columbines), the harmless rebels *Oxalis corniculata* (creeping woodsorrel), and the curvaceous stems of *Geum macrophyllum* (bigleaf avens). Also included were *Fragaria vesca* (wild strawberry), *Nicotiana suaveolens* (Australian tobacco), *Carex grisea* (wood gray sedge), and *Carex elata* 'Aurea' (Bowles' golden sedge).

Container gardening is popular for its boundless creative capacity. Choose any container and proceed to plant passionately. Aesthetic rules apply for a minute, until you've easily concocted something pleasurable and enjoyable no matter if you have fifty pots at your front door or one on your balcony. Consider this encouraging advice to plant something more than just a fiesta of plants exploding in all directions. Dabble with wilder plants, perhaps even weeds, in the confines of your favorite vessel, as a means of exploration before attempting them in open ground. The results can be dramatic and deepen your gardening adventure.

**Choose plants easy to grow from seed or division.** If you're apt to grow plants from seed, you don't need any convincing on this subject. But you could be sitting on a gold mine of plants in your yard already that could easily enjoy a new day in the sun (or shade) when elevated to the status of well-curated container; some might find their way to the container on their own. Compared to the price of many specialty annuals at nurseries, you will likely be dollars ahead by growing your own or patronizing your own propagating stock. Otherwise ordinary plants from your garden's matrix (take the humble, grassy *Carex* or the simple, edible *Fragaria*) can look extraordinary filling or spilling from a container.

**Enjoy the evolution of annual plants from leaf to seed.** I'm fond of growing various *Brassica* (kales, mustards, and the like) in pots in early spring, both for salad nibbling and the freshness they bring to the season. But for all the excitement for their tart, bright leaves, the flowers offer arguably more ecological value serving pollinators such as bees and moths. While many gardeners might associate these acid-yellow flowers with a plant that's stayed too long past its welcome, there is value in celebrating the transition of fast-growing annuals in cool and warm seasons from their emergence to the end of their life cycle.

**Plant single specimens in containers and move them around.** If you're truly gardening with place, you might have to accept that there are some things you just can't grow in your spot of terra firma. But with containers, you can indulge your fetish or fascination for a plant just beyond your reach and use it as an accent in your garden or in concert with other containers. Single specimens, particularly with dramatic leaves or seasonally brief floral displays, can look smart and refined amid wilder beds and borders.

In John Massey's otherwise tidy, traditional garden near his famous Ashwood Nursery, Kingswinford, United Kingdom, this exuberant container unfolded with wild energy featuring *Carex testacea* (New Zealand hair sedge) and *Salvia forsskaolei* (Balkan sage).

## BORDERS AND FOUNDATIONS

You can plant a border almost anywhere, particularly against a foundation or alongside a garage or garden shed. The traditional idea of a border or island bed gives a legible, controlled frame within which to have wilder ambitions. You don't need the total looseness of a meadow in order to cultivate a garden of ecological worth. Borrowing from cottage traditions in Europe, there's plenty of unconscious good ecology happening, including reseeding and dense microclimates created within the planting that minimize the incursion of weeds and provide habitat. Because of the frame and the closeness to the house, the palette might require somewhat tidier shapes and plants.

With so many compositional opportunities for arranging plants in space, the task of planting a border with wilder origins centers on combining plant architectures into a coherent seasonal result year after year. Perhaps this isn't too different from any other traditional approach, but looser players may require precision. Think of plantings like this as layers of a cake using the typologies shared in this book. Use aggressive plants sparingly or avoid altogether; they

will leave a garden too cakey and bulky with not nearly enough frosting. Also consider the width of the border as it affects the use of structural perennials. Too many in a shallow or small space can be visually overwhelming. Conversely, in a larger space, vary the use of these plants to create scrims and veils, which cultivate a sense of depth and curiosity instead of planting what looks like a choir rehearsal. This amounts to good frosting, especially when reseeders tiptoe their way in.

(OPPOSITE PAGE) A brick or stone wall is a common component of a foundation planting, which comes with the added ecological consequence of reflecting heat back into the planting. While this might only have a minor effect on plant physiology, it's worth thinking through the microclimates found in garden spaces alongside the homes and buildings you plant around.

(BOTTOM) Something about this border is audacious: a totally creative planting inspired by the wild nature of plants complete with competitors and ruderals locked in step to botanical tango. As you seek inspiration for your plantings, think about your place on the spectrum between wildness and traditional gardens. The result isn't a compromise as much as an intercession between two important influences.

## Planting Palette for Wild-Inspired Borders

This rather abbreviated palette is principally herbaceous and presents contemporary choices that thrive in warm, sunny conditions with moderate degrees of fertility and consistent drainage. Further, I favor those that either persist with structural value in most climates for much of the growing season or contribute to the spontaneity of the planting at the discretion of the gardener. Plants marked (*) are likely to be somewhat short-lived but proliferate through reseeding.

With an adjacent wall to level the frame, this romantic border is richly layered to illuminate the textures and architectures of *Cotinus* 'Grace' (Grace hybrid smoketree), *Perovskia atriplicifolia* (Russian sage), *Lilium* 'Silk Road' (Silk Road Orienpet lily), and *Macleaya cordata* (plume poppy). Any underlying matrix in late summer is not part of the visual essence, but still present, even as taller leafy perennials shade the ground.

| LAYER | PLANTS | |
|---|---|---|
| **MATRIX** Grasses or groundcovers with cool-season tendencies; herbaceous perennials with basal rosettes. Disperse throughout planting scheme as patchy colonies of many individuals to knit together guilds formed by structural and vignette plants. | *Achnatherum calamagrostis* *Ajania pacifica* *Anthriscus sylvestris* (*) *Carex aurea, bromoides, muskingumensis, oshimensis* *Chrysanthemum* spp. and cultivars *Chrysogonum virginianum* | *Erigeron pulchellus, speciosus* (*) *Molinia caerulea* and cultivars *Pennisetum* spp. and cultivars (*) *Sesleria autumnalis, nitida* *Verbena canadensis* (*) |
| **STRUCTURE** Architectural herbaceous perennials and shrubs, including strongly caespitose grasses; all with coarse, upright habits and varying degrees of visual rigidity. Place to maximize individual plants or small groupings (3–7 per species) scaled to the total proportion of the planting space. | *Agapanthus* spp. and cultivars *Andropogon gerardii* *Amsonia hubrichtii, illustris, tabernaemontana* and cultivars *Cephalaria gigantea* *Chaenomeles* cultivars *Coreopsis tripteris* *Diervilla* spp. and cultivars | *Eragrostis chloromelas* 'Wind Dancer' *Hydrangea paniculata* *Lespedeza thunbergii* *Miscanthus nepalensis* *Panicum virgatum* and cultivars, especially compact selections *Rudbeckia maxima* *Sporobolus heterolepis* *Stipa* spp. |
| **VIGNETTES** Plants with definitive seasonal interest, including scattered emergent reseeders. While a variety of plant architectures are displayed here, most tolerate or withstand modest levels of competition between other garden species, but placement is important to ensure a good fit between the niche and an individual plant's profile. | *Achillea millefolium* *Agastache* spp. and cultivars *Alcea rugosa* *Angelica* spp. and cultivars *Aquilegia* spp. and cultivars *Asclepias* spp. and cultivars *Baptisia* spp. and cultivars *Boehmeria spicata* *Boltonia asteroides* *Coreopsis* spp. and cultivars *Delphinium exaltatum* *Echinacea* spp. and cultivars (*) *Eryngium amethystinum* (*), *bourgatii, giganteum* (*), and *planum* (*) *Eupatorium* and *Eutrochium* spp. and cultivars (*) *Gaura lindheimeri* and cultivars (*) *Geranium* spp. and cultivars *Helenium autumnale* and cultivars *Iris* bearded hybrids *Iris sibirica, spuria* and cultivars *Liatris ligulistylis, pycnostachya* | *Lobelia cardinalis, siphilitica* (*) *Lychnis coronaria* (*) *Macleaya cordata* (*) *Nepeta* × *faassenii, grandiflora, racemosa* *Oenothera tetragona* *Patrinia scabiosifolia* 'Nagoya' (*) *Penstemon barbatus, digitalis* *Phlox paniculata* and cultivars *Rudbeckia* 'American Gold Rush,' *maxima, subtomentosa* 'Little Henry' *Salvia azurea, moorcroftiana* × *indica, nemorosa, nutans* *Sanguisorba canadensis, tenuifolia* and cultivars *Scutellaria incana* *Sidalcea* spp. and cultivars *Silene regia, stellata* (*) *Solidago caesia, drummondii, rigida* *Solidago* 'Loysder Crown' *Symphyotrichum* spp. and cultivars *Thalictrum* spp. and cultivars (*) *Verbena* spp. (*) *Veronicastrum* spp. and cultivars × *Solidaster luteus* |

While annual plantings might seem remote to the idea of New Naturalism, you can think of them as a creative and experimental way to observe how plants grow and change in the microcosm of a single growing season. Further, annual plants aren't merely frivolous to resilient plantings, especially in border settings. They are nature's insurance policy, guaranteeing some element of biodiversity and greenness. What's not to love anyway about the energy and vitality of annuals in full color at the peak of summer (aside from screaming plantings of garish petunias)?

(RIGHT) Reseeding perennials such as *Aquilegia* (columbines) become essential plants for stitching plantings together, unifying various combinations and communities with a serendipitous thread. This degree of self-perpetuation fits the profile of this ruderal, short-lived species. Edit only if necessary; this plant is up to something.

(BOTTOM) In this unselfconscious border, reseeding and spreading have resulted in a dense green skyline seen here from above. Despite similar architectures and niches, a trio of emergents—*Veronicastrum virginicum* 'Fascination,' *Thalictrum dasycarpum*, and *Ageratina altissima* 'Chocolate'—form a dense blockade over the ground and erupt with color from mid- to late summer.

It's only taken Western culture a few hundred years to get comfortable in the mainstream with jibing vegetal and ornamental into one planted space. With space at a premium in the modern residential property, why not take the opportunity to raise a few edibles alongside those supporting other creatures? The synergies between planting for pollinators, which facilitate our food crops, which in turn can build soils just make sense. Take *Raphanus sativus* var. *longipinnatus* (daikon radishes), for instance. Specific strains called tillage radishes have found a purpose in organic agriculture for alleviating compaction in heavy clay soils. If you garden on heavy clay, why not plant these hardworking radishes, edible from leaf to root, even if you never intend to chop them up for a salad? Other cole crops and even grains perform similar services.

(TOP) Even purely annual plantings can offer sugary buffets for pollinators. This design plays up the opportunistic, emergent character of so many annual flowers by forcing them into a competitive, upward dance. Planting by Mark Dwyer.

(TOP) Bolting spikes of *Raphanus sativus* var. *longipinnatus* Ground Hog™ (tillage radishes) play with persistent seedheads of *Penstemon* 'Pocahontas' and *Allium* 'Purple Sensation' in my front yard meadow.

(BOTTOM) This small potager teems with diversity and creativity, casting aside rules for what goes where, intermingling bulbs, edibles, annuals, and perennials; a contemporary garden of useful plants.

(RIGHT) *Planting by Benjamin Futa.*

## Perennials for Bioswales and Damp Conditions

Bioswales, colloquially referred to as rain gardens, are practical plantings that mitigate stormwater in urban landscapes. Many municipalities incentivize their creation, attempting to alleviate demands on underground water and sewer infrastructure. While fashionable for those reasons, so often they lack any kind of ecological practicality to make them functionally and aesthetically successful. The tritest rain gardens amount to a handful of plants adapted to wet soils with the standard mulch or gravel skirt that does little more than wash away when inundated. Effective rain gardens rely on wild precedents such as ephemeral wetlands and marsh edges, transition zones defined by water flow and floodplains, all examples where water levels fluctuate within a growing season and where plant communities naturally have a range of tolerances to extremes such as flooding in spring and seasonal drought in summer. The biological density of these communities is often quite high as expected by the abundance of water and can regenerate quickly after disturbance or stress.

Against a legible, showy hedge of *Hydrangea paniculata*, this roundabout bioswale planting gets away with towering lushness, the plant palette reflecting an ecology of abundant soil moisture: *Eutrochium purpureum* (sweet Joe-Pye weed) with selections of *Molinia* (moorgrass) and *Hibiscus* (rose mallow).

| PLANT NAME | GEOGRAPHIC ORIGIN |
|---|---|
| *Aruncus dioicus* | Eastern North America |
| *Arundo donax* | Middle East |
| *Astilbe chinensis* | Eastern Asia |
| *Canna glauca* | Tropical Americas |
| *Cardamine pratensis* | Europe and Asia |
| *Carex grayi* | Eastern and Midwestern North America |
| *Chelone* spp. | Eastern and Midwestern North America |
| *Deschampsia cespitosa* | North America, Asia, and Europe |
| *Doellingeria umbellata* | Eastern North America |
| *Eupatorium cannabinum* | Europe |
| *Eupatorium perfoliatum* | Eastern North America |
| *Filipendula rubra* | Eastern and Midwestern North America |
| *Filipendula ulmaria* | Europe and Western Asian |
| *Geranium maculatum* | Eastern and Midwestern North America |
| *Geranium pratense* | Europe and Asia |
| *Geum macrophyllum* | Central and Western North America |
| *Geum rivale* | Northern Hemisphere |
| *Hibiscus moscheutos* and cultivars | Eastern North America |
| *Hymenocallis liriosme* | Southeastern North America |
| *Inula magnifica* | Europe |
| *Iris versicolor* | Eastern North America |
| *Lychnis flos-cuculi* | Europe |
| *Persicaria* spp. | Cosmopolitan |
| *Rodgersia pinnata* | Eastern Asia |
| *Rudbeckia fulgida* var. *deamii* | Eastern North America |
| *Sabal minor* | Southeastern North America and Mexico |
| *Sambucus* spp. and cultivars | Northern Hemisphere |
| *Vernonia noveboracensis* | Eastern North America |

# 6  SOFTENING THE HARDSCAPE

**COMPARE THE TURFGRASS** statistic from chapter 5 to the more than 4 million miles of roadways in the United States, the largest total of all countries, which, when combined, account for more than 20.5 million miles of roads across the planet. Reality in the Anthropocene is hard—literally. Asphalt, concrete, and impermeable hardscapes have geological nomenclature such as "urbanite," a curious homonym that has

nothing and everything to do with city dwelling. In the course of developing the modern world, we have managed to inscribe our existence into the Earth's crust and along with it, create challenging situations for basic plant growth.

Urban environments are replete with inhospitable, though not uninhabitable microbiomes for plants. While a rooftop might be the only place you

can grow anything in a dense city, it's not without the stress of wind and intense sunlight. But a whole cottage industry of terrace and balcony designers exists for the purpose of vegetating platforms or rooftops 30 stories in the air. City dwellers with ground-level properties often have a contemptuous relationship with the so-called "hellstrip," the forlorn slice of sometimes balding or foot-trodden turf that fills the verge between the curb and the sidewalk. It's aptly named. Sometimes we even design and create spaces such as patios, stairs, and terraces with hard edges between our space and plantings. At these edges, microclimates form, creating niches for plant diversity that might not exist only a few feet away with richer soils and more competition. Planting these fragment landscapes sews them into the fabric of our communities, embracing challenge as opportunity and encouraging more biodiversity wherever possible.

Ecologically, this eclectic roster of environments runs on stress and disturbance in the form of soil

While obviously not a garden, this shoreline of craggy rocks and deep crevices illustrates the stress some plants endure fulfilling biological programming. An annual, *Eschscholzia californica* (California poppy) paints this harsh reality of the developed world orange and gold.

Species native to glades and limestone bluffs merge to form a wild border growing in and spilling over a limestone wall in a residential garden. *Allium stellatum* (starry onion), *carinatum* ssp. *pulchellum* (keeled garlic), *Crambe maritima* (sea kale), *Phedimus takesimensis*, and *Echinacea tennesseensis* hybrids form an eclectic floral vignette girded by the hazy green matrix of *Sporobolus heterolepis* (prairie dropseed) and *Bouteloua gracilis* 'Blonde Ambition' (Blonde Ambition blue grama grass). Planting design by the author.

fertility, compaction, drainage, foot traffic, urban wildlife, and more. You might even wonder why you would bother planting in these spaces, but nature shows a way. Plants native to midcontinental and montane steppes, glades, rock outcroppings, beaches, ledges, and cliffs include lithophytes, species that grow in or on rocks, and chasmophytes, species that grow in fissures in rocks where organic matter accumulates. Marrying these plants with the built environment's features that ecologically resemble their native haunts matches creative horticulture with a smart analysis of place. As you garden with these plants, pay attention to their conservative architectures once established and avoid disrupting the taproots and exposed, ground-level crowns, which can suffer mechanical damage and occasionally heaving. Cutting back aboveground vegetation in late winter ensures the majority of organic matter leaves the planting system and gives space for new buds to emerge.

Roadside wildflowers have always inspired my planting philosophies, even if all constituents weren't native. In Oregon one summer, I happened upon a ditch full of *Cosmos bipinnatus*, remnants from a former flower seed company's production farm, a floral postcard for ruderality and its short-term value in ecological function.

## GROUND RULES BY LAYERS

### Matrix

Perhaps the most critical component of a streetscape, hellstrip, or curbside planting is a durable or elastic edge. These planting zones, if imagined as three-dimensional units, have large surface edge areas making them prone to continual, if not constant disturbance from sneakers to snowplows. Here, ruderality is essential, even in perennial plantings. Plants that have naturally evolved with disturbance often have annual, biennial, or short perennial life cycles: they either thrive in the face of it or don't hang around long enough for it to matter and reprioritize resources towards the next generation (i.e., seed production). An abundant seedbank helps plantings recover from disturbance, even if a little weeding is necessary—in effect, you're planting and encouraging the fulfillment of life cycles season after season.

### Structure

The opposite scheme—longevity—also has merits, although it might make for slow gardening as you wait for plants to establish themselves to a position of maximal competitive advantage. In climates that favor them, *Agave* and *Yucca* and other members of their family come to mind as examples of undeniably important anchors that hold plantings together with rosette elegance. Opposite the more ruderal elements of the matrix, these stress tolerators invest for the long haul often with deep taproots or woody crowns. They also have a way of directing traffic on account of their size and cutting personalities.

Streetscapes in wetter, temperate zones often feature starry-eyed attempts at canopy with mixed success. Historic trees can cast plenty of shade but can nearly desertify the soil beneath them, leaving it exposed to erosion and degradation. Dry shady conditions illuminate the value of competitive groundcovers, which can have a positive effect on lowering root zone temperatures and increasing soil moisture availability, the kind of green cooling biomass urban areas need more of. If you're set on having a woody plant, choose a small tree or large shrub with an open canopy, something drought-tolerant and modest enough in stature not to overwhelm an already abbreviated space. Examples include *Acer griseum*, *Arctostaphylos* spp., *Cercis* (redbud), *Diervilla lonicera* (bush honeysuckle), *Hamamelis* (witch hazel), small *Prunus* such as *P. maritima*, *Mahonia* spp., and short-statured oaks such as *Quercus gambelii* (Gambel oak) and *Q. prinoides* (dwarf chestnut oak).

### Vignettes

Given the harshness of planting conditions described in this chapter, there are few broad-base prescriptions for thinking about how to fashion vignettes that I haven't already enunciated for the previous two layers. At some point, you'll be thrilled just to find plants that adapt to and thrive in these conditions. In harnessing the courage to plant everywhere, your local knowledge should guide you towards vibrant alternatives to the universal blandness replete throughout acres of built infrastructure. Flowers always help. While novel and invented, these planting communities can recall a sense of wildness that urban centers badly need more of.

Native throughout western North America from up mountains and down to the sea, *Sedum spathulifolium* is a superbly hardy and adaptable groundcover growing from basal rosettes in crevices between small stones or aggregates. Several named forms trade between gardeners and nurseries, often with unique foliar colors that reflect local ecotypes and variation.

Let's rage against the urbanite and stone with beautiful plantings, whether up walls or down stairs. By covering hard, heat-reflecting surfaces with more vegetation, plantings can lower the temperature of the ambient air in cities. Research has shown that surfaces such as glass, concrete, and steel that were covered in plants were 20–45°F (11–25°C) cooler than when the same materials were unshaded. This organic air conditioning reduces energy use, improves air quality, and lowers greenhouse gas emissions. Tree shade has even proven beneficial for slowing the deterioration of concrete. In order to achieve such seemingly lofty goals, plantings must relate to the built environment more effectively than parsley trims pot roast. Petunias and pentas aside, we can aspire to more diverse, nature-forward choices.

In the wild, edge-dwelling is something of a specialty. Many of these wild daredevils resent overhead competition—in resource-constrained environments, competition between species is low—and grow at lower levels of sociality. In conditions where fertility increases, these species tend to experience shorter lifespans. Edges are also heterogeneous, sometimes varying greatly in relatively short order, influenced by drainage, exposure, wind, or other forms of environmental disturbance. You may measure your planting space in inches (centimeters) or feet (meters). Reviewing and studying the place you intend to plant will help you determine what factors to account for. As you begin gardening along these edges, it's sometimes hard to know a planting space from a crack in the wall. Count on plants you use to fill the voids on their own in time, keeping in mind that the tidier they look while doing so, such as with a ground-covering or caespitose habit, will help communicate your intentions and ideas.

(LEFT) A crevice between the stairs and mortared stone wall, covered on one side by *Ficus pumila* (creeping fig), was enough of a toehold for *Euphorbia* 'Blue Haze,' a sterile hybrid, to take root. It's a reminder of the fragility of life on the edge.

(BOTTOM) *Corydalis cheilanthifolia* (fern-leaved fumitory) joins various *Campanula* on this rock wall to fill nearly every imaginable void. While not native to eastern Pennsylvania, where this photo was taken, these adventive plants fill the natural vacuum with minimal human input.

## Planting Palette for Natural Stone and Concrete Edges

Plants listed here thrive in full sun to part shade in average to dry soils, but many can tolerate seasonally wet periods when provided sharp drainage and lean soils. Palettes vary considerably throughout the Northern Hemisphere, but species represented here include horticulturally available novelties that deserve broader application in designed plant communities with stress-driven ecologies.

(RIGHT) While some parts of the world lack rich palettes of spring-flowering bulbs, the near universal appeal and adaptability of species tulips and hybrids, provided ample drainage and an open condition, make for unique habitat combinations.

(BOTTOM) Edges occur everywhere. In maritime climates with more abundant rainfall and higher humidity, walls become homes for weed-suppressing mats of evergreen and semi-evergreen sprawlers such as ferns and *Euonymus fortunei* 'Wolong Ghost.'

| LAYER | PLANTS | |
|---|---|---|
| **MATRIX**<br>Water-wise, caespitose grasses, grasslike plants, and herbaceous perennials with ground-covering or basal rosette architectures. Use patchily throughout the planting as stress and disturbance yield the character of the planting to the structure and vignettes. | *Bouteloua curtipendula, gracilis, hirsuta*<br>*Campanula rotundifolia, poscharskyana*<br>*Carex appalachica, laxiculmis, eburnea, humilis* 'Hexe'<br>*Chiastophyllum oppositifolium*<br>*Eragrostis* spp.<br>*Haberlea* spp.<br>*Herniaria glabra*<br>*Koeleria glauca, macrantha*<br>*Muhlenbergia cuspidata* | *Oryzopsis hymenoides*<br>*Petrophytum caespitosum*<br>*Phlox bifida, nivalis, subulata* and cultivars<br>*Salvia canescens, moorcroftiana* × *indica, officinalis*<br>*Sedum* spp. and cultivars<br>*Sesleria nitida*<br>*Thymus* spp. and cultivars<br>*Tradescantia sillamontana* |
| **STRUCTURE**<br>Water-wise dwarf shrubs, including ground-covering evergreen mats and herbaceous perennials with basal rosettes. Intersperse sporadically throughout the planting in small groupings (3–7 per species) scaled to the total proportion of the planting space or use in larger groupings to hedge or block views. | *Agave* spp. and cultivars<br>*Amorpha canescens, nana, fruticosa*<br>*Arctostaphylos* spp.<br>*Artemisia* spp.<br>*Asparagus verticillatus*<br>*Bergenia* hybrids<br>*Caragana* spp.<br>*Cheilanthes* spp.<br>*Daphne cneorum* and cultivars | *Genista lydia*<br>*Hydrangea arborescens*<br>*Juniperus communis, conferta, horizontalis*<br>*Lavandula angustifolia* and cultivars<br>*Opuntia humifusa, fragilis, phaeacantha, polyacantha*<br>*Pellaea* spp.<br>*Prunus pumila* Jade Parade™, *maritima*<br>*Yucca filamentosa, flaccida, glauca* |
| **VIGNETTES**<br>Water-wise herbaceous perennials generally under 2 feet (0.6 meters) in height, particularly in stressful conditions. Best planted sparsely in small patches or groupings of a 5–9 individuals. Spring-flowering bulbs noted as gap fillers between these isolated groupings (*). | *Allium carinatum* ssp. *pulchellum, cernuum, karataviense* (*), *drummondii, flavum, sphaerocephalon* (*), *stellatum*<br>*Anaphalis* spp.<br>*Antennaria dioica, parviflora, plantaginifolia*<br>*Astragalus* spp.<br>*Calamintha nepeta*<br>*Centranthus ruber*<br>*Crocus* spp. and cultivars (*)<br>*Dracocephalum ruyschiana*<br>*Eriogonum allenii* 'Little Rascal,' *umbellatum*<br>*Eryngium alpinum, campestre, planum*<br>*Heterotheca villosa*<br>*Heuchera americana, cylindrica, hallii, rubescens,* and cultivars<br>*Iris bucharica*(*), *pumila,* and cultivars<br>*Lewisia* spp. and hybrids<br>*Linum* spp. and cultivars | *Manfreda* spp.<br>*Narcissus* spp. and cultivars (*)<br>*Nepeta* spp. and cultivars<br>*Oenothera macrocarpa*<br>*Onobrychis viciifolia*<br>*Penstemon pinifolius*<br>*Plantago* spp.<br>*Pulsatilla patens, vulgaris* and cultivars<br>*Saxifraga* spp. and cultivars<br>*Scabiosa* spp.<br>*Sempervivum* cultivars<br>*Silene virginica*<br>*Tetraneuris acaulis*<br>*Thermopsis rhombifolia*<br>*Tulipa acuminata, clusiana, greigii, praestans, sprengeri* (all *) |

One of my first forays into plantings inspired by wild plant communities began with the idea of a glade, an ecological community that forms in shallow, slivers of organic matter over bedrock. Rich opportunities grow within these rocky hilltops for softening the hard edges of modern landscapes. This inspired my first gravel garden and limestone wall planting, a project rendered to life over the course of a summer in college. While I was principally trying to recreate a plant community to study in garden conditions, I discovered a whole new palette of stress-tolerant perennials and opportunistic annuals, including some lurking within my own local flora. These photographs show the planting in its early years before some of the grasses formed hazy swards in areas where the gravel couldn't hold back the mild fertility of a former lawn.

| LAYER | PLANTS |
|---|---|
| **MATRIX**<br>The stress of the ground plane, a layer of pea gravel, grit, and limestone shards, was principally designed as the mechanism by which to hold the planting ecologically accountable. The pillowy mounds described in the vignettes section accessorized this purpose in the first few years until the grasses filled in. | *Bouteloua curtipendula*<br>*Schizachyrium scoparium* |
| **STRUCTURE**<br>A handful of leafy perennials, mostly with peak ornamental displays in late summer or fall, provided a transition between the floral confetti of the vignettes and beige stones. | *Eryngium yuccifolium*<br>*Hylotelephium* cultivars<br>*Solidago drummondii* |
| **VIGNETTES**<br>The floral components were loose, emergent perennials with airy shapes and mounded, leafy perennials with persistent stems and foliage. The contrast between these two, further joined by a handful of reseeding annuals that also grouted the cracks in the dry stacked limestone, formed tight guilds of color and interest from midsummer through early autumn. | *Anemone multifida*<br>*Callirhoe involucrata*<br>*Capnoides sempervirens*<br>*Centaurea montana* 'Presley's Blue Hawaii'<br>*Helenium amarum*<br>*Linum perenne*<br>*Monarda bradburiana*<br>*Opuntia polyacantha*<br>*Phemeranthus calycinus, rugospermus*<br>*Pycnanthemum tenuifolium*<br>*Saponaria* × *lempergii* 'Max Frei'<br>*Symphyotrichum ericoides, pilosum* |

(OPPOSITE PAGE) Grown as an exotic adornment for this staircase at Mount Stewart in Northern Ireland, *Beschorneria yuccoides* (Mexican lily) thrives in the sharply draining microclimate offered by a granite stairs and walls, hearkening to its wild origins.

(TOP RIGHT) Many gardeners wish they could grow moss and go to great lengths to coax them into existence. Some just get lucky. Influenced by coastal weather and mild temperatures throughout the year, mosses, ferns, and *Ophiopogon planiscapus* trim the hard edges of this stone staircase.

(BOTTOM LEFT) Some gardeners are determined to grow unusual plants, even constructing and repurposing urbanite to build crevice gardens as seen here at Juniper Level Botanic Garden (Raleigh, NC, USA). These horticultural concoctions of cliffside dwellings for chasmophytic plants (plants that grow in chasms or cracks) amount to living experiments that explore plants from tough places in the designed, novel ecology of the urban wildness.

(BOTTOM RIGHT) Nature's crevice communities can look gardenesque upon close inspection as in this tightly woven guild of *Penstemon glaber* (sawsepal beardtongue), *Arctostaphylos uva-ursi* (kinnikinnick), *Koeleria macrantha* (junegrass), and even *Clematis columbiana* var. *tenuiloba* (rock clematis).

In his book *American Eden*, author Wade Graham proffered that the mark of a landscape architect is anywhere a skateboard can go. While seemingly pejorative, it's what professionals are so often called to do as they design neighborhoods, office complexes, and parking lots. If you live in an urban area, chances are you have a curb in your midst; it's a fundamental truth in a system designed to reroute water from the surface to underground. Take a walk through many neighborhoods in dense urban areas and you'll eventually find a gardener whose passion for plants barely recognizes the street as a boundary. Perhaps you even garden alongside one; doing so is an art in and of itself. Curbside gardens—"streetscapes" by a more architectural parlance—extend the depth and density of ecological plantings to the edge of public space, a form of outreach and education. For all its challenges, the curb presents beautiful opportunities to build community and create awareness for all the wilder gardening throughout the rest of your property.

Research shows that beautiful streetscapes increase perceptions of safety, spontaneous interactions between neighbors, and walkability. These are the kinds of gardens we need more of and everywhere. Beyond the human condition, these ecologically productive greenspaces create ribbons of life running through our communities, tiny threads added up alongside gardens and parks providing corridors for insects, birds, and mammals to travel. They also require relatively small investments to plant on account of their limited square footage. As a contribution goes, why not extend vibrant vegetation as a welcome mat for your neighbors and passersby?

The conditions are unforgiving, spanning the gamut from heavy and compacted to loose and gravelly soils, neither of which at first blush might give rise to much life at all. The soil and ambient air temperatures are often higher by a few degrees, too, thanks to such close proximity to a baking slab of asphalt, which introduces even more stress to plants. But these aren't conditions to shy away from. In fact, there's an ample palette of plants ready to seize the opportunity, even if they don't live forever. Designing and planting at the curb tests all applications of New Naturalism as we harness the power of plants in place to create a self-perpetuating, waterwise, resilient garden.

The Josephine Streetscape at Denver Botanic Garden, USA, presents a site-specific, climate-resonant planting that illuminates the opportunities for ecology in the remnant, interstitial vacancies in the built environment. Planting by Kevin Williams.

(TOP) Early successional grasses such as *Eragrostis spectabilis* (purple lovegrass) and other members of that genus function ably in disturbed conditions where their tendency to reseed allows them to perpetuate. In drier, seasonally arid climates, they can become weedy.

(LEFT) As the built environment transitions into the landscape, it's fun to watch what colonizes the verge, like these *Carex laxiculmis* (glaucous sedge) and various *Heuchera* seedlings in New York City, a potential inspiration and cue from nature as to what's working in this place.

## Planting Palette for Hellstrips in Open Exposures

Plants listed here thrive in disturbance-prone conditions with well-drained soils and open exposures, including some light shade. Selections require few investments after establishment thriving with good salt tolerance. Many plants on this palette would thrive in green roof applications.

This curbside planting outside of Denver Botanic Gardens (Denver, CO, USA) exuberantly illustrates the potential for habitat-driven gardens with an articulated color palette from a xeric palette. Planting by Kevin Williams.

| LAYER | PLANTS |
|---|---|
| **MATRIX**<br>Water-wise, caespitose grasses, grasslike plants, and ground-covering herbaceous perennials and reliable self-sowers. Disperse throughout planting scheme as patchy colonies of many individuals to knit together guilds formed by structural and vignette plants or use in large colonies to fill space. | *Acorus gramineus*<br>*Anemone canadensis*<br>*Bigelowia nuttallii*<br>*Bouteloua curtipendula, gracilis* 'Blonde Ambition'<br>*Briza media*<br>*Callirhoe involucrata*<br>*Carex albicans, flacca*<br>*Chasmanthium latifolium*<br>*Geum fragarioides*<br>*Melica ciliata*<br>*Mentha longifolia*<br>*Monarda bradburiana, didyma, fistulosa, luteola*<br>*Panicum virgatum* (dwarf cultivars)<br>*Rubus calycinoides*<br>*Ruellia humilis*<br>*Saxifraga stolonifera*<br>*Schizachyrium scoparium* and cultivars<br>*Sedum* spp. and cultivars |
| **STRUCTURE**<br>Stress-tolerant, architectural perennials, dwarf shrubs, and small trees. Intersperse sporadically throughout the planting in small groupings (3–7 per species) scaled to the total proportion of the planting space or use in larger groupings to hedge or block views. | *Amelanchier laevis*<br>*Asimina triloba*<br>*Betula nigra* 'Little King'<br>*Cercis canadensis*<br>*Eryngium agavifolium, yuccifolium*<br>*Hamamelis* spp. and cultivars<br>*Hylotelephium* cultivars<br>*Hypericum kalmianum, prolificum*<br>*Kniphofia* spp. and cultivars<br>*Mahonia repens*<br>*Prunus besseyi*<br>*Rhus typhina* 'Bailtiger'<br>*Solidago drummondii, rigida, rugosa*<br>*Symphyotrichum oblongifolium* 'Fanny,' 'October Skies,' 'Raydon's Favorite' |
| **VIGNETTES**<br>Water-wise herbaceous perennials generally under 2 feet (0.6 meters) in height. Best planted sparsely in small patches or groupings of 5–9 individuals. | *Agastache rupestris* and cultivars, 'Blue Boa,' Kudos series, Poquito series<br>*Anemone multifida*<br>*Callirhoe digitata*<br>*Coreopsis lanceolata, palmata, rosea, verticillata*<br>*Epilobium canum* and cultivars<br>*Helenium amarum*<br>*Pycnanthemum tenuifolium*<br>*Salvia argentea, azurea, blepharophylla, chamaedryoides, greggii, microphylla, pachyphylla* |

This streetscape adjacent to Denver Botanic Gardens shimmers in silver and gray alongside a busy street. Stumbling through a few summers ago en route to a coffee shop, I marveled at its wild spirit and reality, featuring both stress-tolerant competitors such as *Artemisia ludoviciana* (Louisiana sage) and true-grit annuals such as *Euphorbia marginata* (snow-on-the-mountain) and *Helianthus annuus* (annual sunflower). It was a bold and daring gesture in a planting space only 3 feet (1 meter) wide. Grown from a combination of plugs and seeds sown into a 4-inch (10-cm) layer of sand, sometimes barely covering the exposed tree roots of the street trees, the space evolved quickly with ecology of its components to its advantage. Given the anticipated regular disturbance, gardening amounts to monitoring and managing how the planting responds.

Hellstrips, the most abundant and least utilized community garden, are heavily influenced by disturbance, including everything from street maintenance equipment to humans and dogs. They straddle the edge between the shade of trees, houses, and maybe any glimpse of light that reaches the ground, even if only for a few hours a day. These edge conditions as we learned in chapter 1 have the potential to support a wide range of plant diversity because of the many different kinds of niches available. On this residential street, meadow grasses and perennials join stress-tolerant succulents and ephemeral bulbs to form an eclectic palette in a novel, personable garden.

The highly competitive perennial *Artemisia ludoviciana* (Louisiana sage) grows into larger and larger areas, which was an asset in the early years of this planting as it virtually eliminated the need for routine weeding. The biennial or short-lived perennial *Monarda punctata* (horsemint) features as a classic ruderal, gap-filling profile with plants recruited annually from the seedbank as opportunity permits.

In spring, the assorted green textures from grasses and newly awakened perennials form a composed matrix from which *Hyacinthoides hispanica* (Spanish bluebells) and *Euphorbia rigida* (stiff spurge) appear.

(TOP) Planted and grown by Scott Weber.

(LEFT) *Rhus typhina* 'Bailtiger' (Tiger Eyes™ cutleaf sumac) anchors the corner block planting, capturing the light for an illuminating backdrop to looser, finer textures.

## Crack-Wise Plants

Have you ever stopped to notice the motley crew of plants growing in the cracks of sidewalks? If you have, you're not alone. As hardscapes fracture and falter in the built environment, they create opportunities for biological activity. Think about how you might encourage the more horticulturally personable of these otherwise derided weeds. What's a weed anyway, but a brazen opportunist? Who knows, you might discover new filler in the process or take the opportunity to celebrate the wabi-sabi ways of wayward plants.

In this small patio off the back step at Great Dixter, phrases such as "unkempt chaos" and "botanical bedlam" seem more appropriate than "garden." *Campanula, Dierama, Carex, Iris* and more—all adventitious from the surrounding garden—populate the crevices between each paver for a fortuitous, self-determining plant community.

| PLANT NAME | GEOGRAPHIC ORIGIN OF SPECIES |
| --- | --- |
| *Bidens bipinnata* | North America |
| *Campanula portenschlagiana* | Europe |
| *Campanula poscharskyana* | Europe |
| *Cichorium intybus* | Europe and Asia |
| *Cymbalaria muralis* | Europe |
| *Erigeron annuus* | North America |
| *Erigeron karvinskianus* | Mexico and Central America |
| *Erigeron philadelphicus* | North America |
| *Fumaria officinalis* | Europe, Asia, and Northern Africa |
| *Impatiens capensis* | Eastern North America |
| *Linaria purpurea* | Europe |
| *Linaria vulgaris* | Europe and Asia |
| *Oenothera biennis* | North America |
| *Phemeranthus* spp. | Americas |
| *Pseudofumaria lutea* | Europe |
| *Ranunculus sceleratus* | Circumpolar |
| *Silene latifolia* | Europe |
| *Symphyotrichum pilosum* | North America |
| *Tragopogon dubius* | Europe and Asia |
| *Verbascum* spp. and hybrids | Europe, Africa, and Asia |

# 7      GREEN SHADE AND DAPPLED EDGES

**VOLUMES EXIST FOR** guiding gardeners to success in the dimness of green shade. On an increasingly warming planet, the future of life as we know it might well be underneath the green shade of the trees we plant today. Your most forward-looking act as gardener is to plant a tree, preferably a native, so that the life you give it in the garden might yield more in the decades to come.

Planting trees needs no extensive enunciation. Whatever you choose, smart tree selections create multi-dimensional habitats for everything from birds and tree-dwelling mammals that nest and feed in their canopies to the invertebrates that live in the leafy detritus underneath them. Studies of woodland ecosystems have shown that a developed canopy layer can increase wildlife diversity by 3 to 15 times as many

species compared to shrub and ground-cover diversity, respectively.

If you don't garden with existing canopy where this richness of life no doubt already exists, you needn't waste any time. Fast-growing trees such as *Betula* (birches) are common choices for quick canopy, although most species that grow fast usually die young. Ask yourself how long a birch tree lives or recall the oldest one you've seen and you would be hard pressed to consider one that made it more than a quarter century. Conversely, noble trees with admirable statures such as *Quercus* (oak) don't spring up overnight. I proffer no judgement on the growth rate of trees and how far off in the future real shade might loom; this book by now has probably underscored my fervent belief that every plant has its place, whether it's in your garden or not.

This woodland edge planting adjacent to a pergola at Chanticleer Garden (Wayne, PA, USA) thrives under the dappled, angular shade of *Betula populifolia* (gray birch). An abundant carpet of reseeding *Phlox divaricata* (woodland phlox) ties together drifts of *Delphinium tricorne* (wild larkspur), various tulips, and other ephemerals.

In this managed woodland near a residential development, this stand of oaks was initially planted densely to encourage the population's natural self-thinning over time, which resulted in individual trees growing tall and with narrower canopies than if each tree had been planted to develop as a specimen. While it depends on the species, planting small trees in the home landscape at higher densities fosters greater competition and narrower canopy development and allows trunks to become important aesthetic features of understory plantings.

The choreography of plantings in shade is critical to account for the evolution of niches in a single growing season. Here the foliage of *Sanguinaria canadensis* (bloodroot) (center) is starting to flag in late spring as an ample cast of ferns, various *Geranium* (cranesbill), and *Hakonechloa macra* (Japanese forest grass) assume its niche, leaving no gaps in the planting.

The business of shade is had between trees, but not equitably. Evergreens run roughshod with ever-present canopies and annual needle drops that can make gardening beneath them interesting. All trees have natural flares where the roots and trunk meet the ground, but some species such as *Acer* (maple), *Salix* (willow), and nearly all *Magnolia* species have dense roots just below the soil surface that can create a dry microclimate and limit the extent of understory plantings. Trees leaf out at different times, influencing how much light and when it reaches the understory, something critical even for species adapted to horticultural darkness. Many woodland ephemerals wake up in response to soil temperature and steadily increasing daylength, perceptions of which require that some light starts to coax them from beneath their bedding of fallen leaves. Knowing your trees and studying how they influence place will lead you toward a solution for planting them a skirt.

Some plants thrive simply because shade exists. But some plants thrive on the degree of shadiness, with only a little (such as *Anemone hupehensis* (Japanese anemone)) or a lot (*Aspidistra* (cast iron plants) or *Dryopteris* (wood ferns)). Soil fertility and soil depth influence woodland plantings; consider the differences between a woodland on a low floodplain versus one on top of a rocky bluff. Consider the wind that might roar through the trees on that upland bluff, particularly in spring before leafy canopies do much umbrella-ing. If you have a wooded slope to plant, consider yourself lucky. Shade is only barely unifying in these varied situations, which the eclectic palettes in this chapter reflect.

Slice the prototype of a woodland from the shadiest peak of its canopy to its sunniest edge and you'd end up with layers of canopy trees, understory trees and shrubs, vines, upright and ground-covering herbaceous perennials, and roots. The three-layer typology in this book fits perfectly. Shade is often densest under the thickest canopy and most permeating towards the edge, though shifts in topography can change the extent of the zone of shadiness. Keep in mind that the more structural shrubs you plant to bridge the canopy with understory, the more shade you create for the lowest level of the garden. If this is your goal, perhaps to embrace an existing hedge or to account for a collection of shrubs that form some essence of the garden, so be it. This will, however, place some limitations on the palette for maximal shade tolerance.

Through the ideas and precedents offered here, some mastered only by ducking under limbs and peering into the world beneath, I hope you find ample inspiration to reinvent the hosta ghetto into something more diverse, more interesting, and with heightened ecological flair.

## GROUND RULES BY LAYERS

### Matrix

Most plants that occupy this layer in wild shaded situations are tough and vigorous, often colonizers keenly adapted to local conditions. For making gardens, this area-covering tendency counts as an asset and creates a strong patchwork within which emergent colonies and communities of other plants in the vignettes layer may emerge. Whatever you do, plant generously to ensure a strong initial matrix forms to support the planting in the years ahead. These plants, perhaps more than any other part of the landscape, do a lion's share of work in relatively stressful (low-light) conditions. While the edges can promote greater levels of plant diversity, you don't want a majority of this diversity represented by plants you didn't intend to have in your garden. In the palettes, I've separated extensive groundcovers from plants with lower social tendencies given the somewhat major differences for using and layering them.

### Structure

In the understory of many residential plantings, shrubs will rarely play a central role if you want to promote greater light and diversity. This chapter features several lists dedicated to shrubs and small trees to account for their overall absence in the understory. Instead, with a cathedral of trees overhead, the understory zone should teem with architectural perennials with strong lines that convey an undulation and herbaceous topography to the ground layer. This herbaceous scaffold will increase the legibility and the vibrancy of the vignettes.

### Vignettes

In the understory, a well-choreographed scene unfolds as the result of natural lifecycles of woodland ephemerals and perennials coloring up the ground early while light is plentiful, only to retreat once shade returns. You can account for these summer gaps with perennials that form leafy canopies over their dormant neighbors, the latter coming into view as the former fade away. Further, many spring-flowering perennials native to woodlands have distinct niches within the community, some favoring deep shade and minimal disturbance while most others adapt to edges and varying degrees of light. Some of these dynamics depend on the shape of the planting area and its dimensions, but it's good to follow local and near-native precedents for the major, charismatic species of the planting in order to achieve something visually harmonious and ecologically realistic.

## UNDERSTORY

If you begin with an established canopy, the understory becomes the canvas for your planting efforts. As you compose your new shade garden, keep the layers distinct and legible, something you'll manage over time with pruning as understory shrubs stretch toward the light. It's easy for woods to blur into thickets and brush when too many shrubs or small trees obscure the nobility of the taller canopy. In your study of place, consider the number and nature of openings beneath and between larger trees. This will guide your choice of small trees or large shrubs, particularly with respect to their canopy sizes and shapes as if you were fitting them into the greater puzzle. Landscape architect Frederick Law Olmsted was clever about layering the darker, bolder outlines of some shrubs in the foreground while utilizing more herbaceous structure in the backdrop to create an optical illusion of a space seeming larger than it was. Our eyes get used to the choir rehearsal effect—tallest to smallest—so anything that disrupts this predictable layering engenders new perceptions of space.

(TOP)  At the edge of a native woodland with a canopy of *Quercus macrocarpa* (bur oak) and *Carya ovata* (shagbark hickory), this cozy shade planting is home to an ample reseeding community of *Phlox divaricata* (woodland phlox), *Sanicula odorata* (common black snakeroot), and *Viola sororia* (common violet), all native to the site and coaxed into the fold over several years. Nonnative garden perennials join various species of *Carex* (sedge) to round out this novel, designed, and self-perpetuating plant community. Planted and grown by the author.

(RIGHT)  Sublimely composed, this planting in shade masters every niche with effective contrasts between plant architectures and subtle color coordination. In humus-rich, moist soil with some light penetration to the ground, plants such as *Rodgersia aesculifolia* (fingerleaf rodgersia) excel both as a plant for structure and vignettes.

# Planting Palette for the Understory

Shade-tolerant plants listed here represent functional choices for northern temperate zones in soils ranging from dry to wet with manageable sizes best adapted for home-scale planting projects. Plants in both columns straddle the verge in tolerances, not necessarily to either extreme.

Even at the shady margins of this shade garden, spring tidings lurk in the form of *Tulipa sylvestris* (woodland tulip) with its gently nodding bells that perennialize in loamy soils.

| LAYER | SOIL MOISTURE | |
| --- | --- | --- |
| | **WET TO MEDIUM WET** | **MEDIUM DRY TO DRY** |
| **MATRIX**<br>Spreading habits, basal rosettes, and leafy rounded mounds. For groundcovering, space-filling habits, see palettes in the next section. Disperse throughout planting scheme as patchy colonies of many individuals to knit together guilds formed by structural and vignette plants. Use proportionately more than plants from either of the other categories. | *Adiantum capillus-veneris, pedatum, venustum*<br>*Athyrium* spp.<br>*Carex elata* 'Aurea,' *sprengelii*<br>*Carex morrowii*<br>*Clintonia andrewsiana, borealis, umbellulata*<br>*Geranium* spp. and cultivars<br>*Milium effusum* 'Aureum'<br>*Omphalodes cappadocica* | *Adiantum capillus-veneris, pedatum, venustum*<br>*Allium neapolitanum, victorialis*<br>*Athyrium* spp.<br>*Cyclamen* spp.<br>*Heuchera richardsonii, villosa* and cultivars<br>*Hypericum calycinum*<br>*Iris cristata, tectorum*<br>*Omphalodes cappadocica*<br>*Pachyphragma integrifolium*<br>*Phlox divaricata, stolonifera*<br>*Sedum ternatum*<br>*Umbilicus oppositifolius* |

(*continued*)

| LAYER | SOIL MOISTURE | |
|---|---|---|
| | WET TO MEDIUM WET | MEDIUM DRY TO DRY |
| **STRUCTURE**<br><br>Primarily architectural herbaceous perennials; vertical, upright habits or heightened visual dominance. Place to maximize individual plants or small groupings (3–7 per species) scaled to the total proportion of the planting space. | *Actaea* spp. and cultivars<br>*Bletilla striata* and cultivars<br>*Cypripedium* spp. and cultivars<br>*Diphylleia cymosa*<br>*Disporum* spp. and cultivars<br>*Dryopteris* spp.<br>*Galax aphylla*<br>*Glaucium palmatum*<br>*Helianthus decapetalus*<br>*Iris versicolor* and cultivars<br>*Osmunda* spp.<br>*Polygonatum* spp. and hybrids<br>*Polystichum* spp.<br>*Rodgersia* spp. and cultivars<br>*Thalictrum aquilegiifolium, delavayi, rochebrunianum*<br>*Veratrum album, californicum, nigrum, virginicum* | *Athyrium* spp. and cultivars<br>*Clematis heracleifolia* and cultivars<br>*Comptonia peregrina*<br>*Helleborus* spp. and cultivars<br>*Hosta* spp. and cultivars<br>*Iris foetidissima*<br>*Maianthemum oleraceum, racemosum*<br>*Matteuccia struthiopteris*<br>*Paeonia daurica, emodi, ostii*<br>*Podophyllum hexandrum, pleianthum, peltatum*<br>*Polygonatum* spp. and hybrids<br>*Polystichum* spp.<br>*Pulmonaria* spp. and cultivars<br>*Rodgersia* spp. and cultivars<br>*Uvularia grandiflora, concatenate*<br>*Yucca flaccida, louisianensis* |
| **VIGNETTES**<br><br>Plants with definitive seasonal interest, either evenly distributed for large thematic effects or in tight combinations with great artistic license; includes ephemerals. | *Aconitum* spp. and cultivars<br>*Anemone hupehensis, japonica*<br>*Arisaema* spp. and cultivars<br>*Begonia grandis*<br>*Camassia* spp. and cultivars<br>*Cardamine concatenate, douglassii, diphylla, pratensis*<br>*Corydalis* spp. and cultivars<br>*Deschampsia cespitosa*<br>*Dodecatheon meadia*<br>*Erythronium* spp. and cultivars<br>*Fritillaria meleagris*<br>*Hylomecon japonicum*<br>*Lamprocapnos spectabilis*<br>*Lathyrus vernus*<br>*Mertensia virginica*<br>*Primula bulleyana, japonica, vulgaris* and hybrids<br>*Tricyrtis* spp. and cultivars<br>*Trillium* spp. | *Aconitum* spp. and cultivars<br>*Anemone hupehensis, japonica*<br>*Aquilegia* spp. and cultivars<br>*Arisaema* spp. and cultivars<br>*Begonia grandis*<br>*Campanula persicifolia*<br>*Campanulastrum americanum*<br>*Dicentra canadensis, cucullaria, eximia*<br>*Fritillaria thunbergii, uva-vulpis*<br>*Gentiana asclepiadea*<br>*Gillenia trifoliata*<br>*Hacquetia epipactis*<br>*Hepatica* spp. and cultivars<br>*Lathyrus vernus*<br>*Mertensia virginica*<br>*Sanguinaria canadensis*<br>*Thalictrum dioicum, thalictroides*<br>*Tricyrtis* spp. and cultivars |

(LEFT AND RIGHT) A pair of Eastern North American natives *Spigelia marilandica* (woodland pinkroot) and *Scutellaria incana* (hoary skullcap) are classic understory, edge-thriving perennials with architectures and midsummer bloom times adapted both to sun and shade. Both make excellent companions in guilds with average to moist soils.

In this residential border, natives and nonnatives intermingle in a layered planting with highly compatible plant architectures, including a matrix of various selections of *Geranium* (cranesbill) with leafy mounded habits and *Carex* (sedge) with grassy, caespitose habits.

This hillside planting at Chanticleer Gardens (Wayne, PA, USA) synthesizes multiple wild archetypes into a planting that will grow more shaded as it patinates with age. In these juvenile years, a *Carex* (sedge) and *Nassella tenuissima* (Mexican feather grass) understory features waves of colorful perennials tumbling down the dappled slope including *Silene virginica* (fire pink), *Monarda bradburiana* (eastern horsemint), and *Aruncus aethusifolius* (dwarf goatsbeard).

*Eurybia divaricata* (white woodland aster) forms frothy, cloud-like mounds of flowers in late summer, illustrating that the matrix of understory plantings isn't always green.

# CASE STUDY

This bog garden in a maritime climate on the shaded edge of a pond features a robust palette of competitors romping around in fertile, wet conditions amid a chorus of singing amphibians. The composition embraces introduced and adventive flora with local natives.

| LAYER | PLANTS |
|---|---|
| **MATRIX**<br>In wet situations, it's easy for highly competitive, groundcovering and tall emergent perennials to occupy areas by clonal structures. | *Equisetum arvense*<br>*Ranunculus repens* |
| **STRUCTURE**<br>Set inside a canopy of smaller trees, a majority of the planting receives around 4 hours of daily sunlight during the peak growing season, favoring bold and leafy perennials that can stretch toward the light and create dramatic, horticultural trusses that give framework for the vignettes. | *Aruncus aethusifolius*<br>*Carex pendula*<br>*Gunnera manicata*<br>*Hakonechloa macra* 'Aureola'<br>*Iris × pseudacorus*<br>*Libertia grandiflora*<br>*Lysichiton americanus*<br>*Polystichum munitum* |
| **VIGNETTES**<br>The floral layer waltzed from spring into summer with ground-hugging perennials that formed a pseudo-matrix along exposed edges. | *Oxalis oregana*<br>*Primula japonica* |

## Small Understory Trees for Residential Plantings

In urban settings, gardeners rarely have the opportunity to conceive of a canopy. Instead, gardening often takes places underneath established trees, where more modest gestures frame spaces for living and habitats.

The following plants are examples of small trees or large, arborescent shrubs that fit well into structural planting layers in concert with taller woody plants.

| PLANT NAME | GEOGRAPHIC ORIGIN | AVERAGE HEIGHT (FT/M) |
| --- | --- | --- |
| *Acer palmatum* | Eastern Asia | 10–20 feet (3–6 m) |
| *Acer pensylvanicum* | Eastern North America | 15–25 feet (4.6–7.6 m) |
| *Amelanchier* spp. and cultivars | North America | 15–40 feet (4.5–12 m) |
| *Asimina triloba* | North America | 15–20 feet (4.5–6 m) |
| *Carpinus caroliniana* | Eastern North America | 20–35 feet (6–10.6 m) |
| *Cercis canadensis* | Eastern North America | 20–35 feet (6–10.6 m) |
| *Chionanthus* spp. | Eastern North America and Eastern Asia | 3–25 feet (1–7.6 m) |
| *Cornus* spp. | North America and Asia | 10–20 feet (3–6 m) |
| *Ficus* 'Brown Turkey' | Middle East | 10–12 feet (3–3.7 m) |
| *Heptacodium miconioides* | Eastern Asia | 15–20 feet (4.5–6 m) |
| *Magnolia sieboldii* | Northeast Asia | 10–15 feet (3–4.5 m) |
| *Malus* 'Cinzam' (Cinderella) | Cultivated | 6–8 feet (1.8–2.4 m) |
| *Oxydendrum arboreum* | Southeast North America | 15–30 feet (4.6–9 m) |
| *Prunus* spp. | North America and Asia | 10–30 feet (3–9 m) |
| *Quercus prinoides* | Eastern North America | 3–12 feet (1–3.6 m) |
| *Stewartia monadelpha* | Japan and Korea | 20–25 feet (6–7.6 m) |
| *Styrax* spp. | North America and Asia | 10–20 feet (3–6 m) |
| *Viburnum prunifolium* | Eastern North America | 12–15 feet (3.7–4.6 m) |
| *Xanthoceras sorbifolium* | Asia | 10–20 feet (3–6 m) |

## Shrubs for Edges and Hedges

Not all landscapes are so categorical or offer discrete places to plant template gardens. The edges and boundaries often require thinking outside traditional planting plans, particularly with so many of them prevalent in the built environment: shaded sidewalks, raised beds behind a building, property lines abutting natural areas, and more. The man-made hedgerow, the living property boundaries between agricultural fields and suburban developments, provides a pseudo-natural precedent that supports animal movement, foraging, and nesting.

Overlapping conditions of exposure and soil create niche opportunities for dynamic, durable planting schemes that thrive in the microclimates between two different areas. Edges also provide pragmatic opportunities for creating pathways, which simply inscribe the natural disturbance into landscape use, hedges that block or frame views, and mitigate noise. Shrubs are the principal component of these interstitial plant communities but selecting them for this capacity requires rethinking shrubs as many gardeners know them. The following list includes shrubs with carefree architectures and vigorous growth habits suited for informal hedging.

| PLANT NAME | PLANT DIMENSIONS (H × W) | GEOGRAPHIC ORIGIN OF SPECIES |
| --- | --- | --- |
| *Aesculus parviflora* | 10 × 15 feet (3 × 4.5 m) | Southeastern North America |
| *Amelanchier laevis* | 15–40 feet (4.5–12 m) tall and wide | Eastern North America |
| *Aronia* spp. and cultivars | Variable based on selection | Eastern North America |
| *Baccharis* spp. | 10–15 feet (3–4.5 m) tall and wide | Americas |
| *Calycanthus floridus* | 6–9 feet (1.8–2.7 m) tall and wide | Eastern North America |
| *Caragana arborescens* | 15 feet (4.5 m) tall and wide | Asia |
| *Cornus alternifolia* | 15–20 feet (4.5–6 m) tall and wide | North America |
| *Corylus* spp. | Variable based on selection | Northern Hemisphere |
| *Craetagus monogyna* | 19 × 26 feet (6 × 8 m) tall and wide | Europe and Asia |
| *Craetagus viridis* | 16–50 feet (5–15 m) tall and wide | North America |
| *Forsythia* spp. and cultivars | 8 × 6 feet (2.5 × 1.8 m) | Europe and Asia |
| *Frangula alnus* | 10–20 feet (3–6 m) tall and wide | Europe and Asia |
| *Hamamelis* spp. and cultivars | Variable based on selection | North America and Asia |
| *Lindera* spp. and cultivars | 6–12 feet (1.8–3.7 m) tall and wide | North America and Asia |
| *Prunus angustifolia* | 4–20 feet (1.2–6 m) tall and wide | North America |
| *Prunus spinosa* | 16 × 13 feet (5 × 4 m) | Europe and Asia |
| *Ribes* spp. and cultivars | 4–8 feet (1.2–2.5 m) tall and wide | North America |
| *Salix purpurea* cultivars | 10–20 feet (3–6 m) tall and wide | Europe and Asia |
| *Sassafras albidum* | 30 × 40 feet (9 × 12 m) | Eastern North America |
| *Sheperdia argentea* | 10 feet (3 m) tall and wide | Western North America |
| *Symphoricarpos* spp. and cultivars | 3–6 feet (1–2 m) tall and wide | North America and Asia |
| *Viburnum dentatum* | 6–10 feet (2–3 m) tall and wide | Eastern North America |
| *Viburnum dilatatum* | 10 × 8 feet (3 × 2.5 m) | Asia |
| *Viburnum nudum* | 5–12 feet (1.5–3.7 m) tall and wide | Eastern North America |

## THE GREEN TAPESTRY

With so many opportunities to weave together the woodland floor, the ground-covering matrix plants deserve special treatment to underscore their significance and value. This ultimate ground layer may not simply be spackle that holds the planting together, such as in the understory palette earlier in this chapter. In some gardens, it is the principle planting, either due to lack of space or a desire to create a highly functional groundcover without a lot of fuss. In some heavily forested regions of the world, this cohort of plants plays a significant role in the ecosystem and may contain a number of locally charismatic species. This section features plants with higher orders of sociality that grow into beautiful tapestries. As you make selections and assemble a planting palette, prepare to order larger quantities of plants to effectively fill the space. As for spacing, consider that many plants with ground-covering habits grow in all directions to form colonies; you're planting the mother that will give rise to a network of plantlets. Each species does this at a unique rate and with different vegetative structures,

so it's important to consider these fine-scale compatibilities for long-term success. Luckily, most of these competitors have extended lifespans in gardens because they can just keep growing. If disturbance damages some portion of the network, it can regenerate and grow away from the point of disturbance or repair it through new adventitious growth.

(TOP) In this woodland edge garden with a mature canopy of *Pseudotsuga menziesii* (Douglas fir), tapestries of plants colonize the edges in hierarchical fashion from the largest and most textural *Rodgersia* to the creeping mat of *Cymbalaria muralis* (Kenilworth ivy).

(LEFT) In dappled conditions on soils ranging from wet to dry, members of the saxifrage family can form extensive colonies of small, tidy clumps that overlap to form a continuous green carpet as shown here with *Mitella diphylla* (bishop's cap).

Many woodland saxifrage family members such as *Tellima grandiflora* (bigflower tellima) work ably well as threads in the green tapestry, clumping for a tidy appearance and gently colonizing areas via short stolons that extend the clumps in all directions.

On a large hillside slope with a dappled canopy, interwoven matrices of spreading plants help hold the soil in place. *Onoclea sensibilis* (sensitive fern) and *Polygonatum odoratum* 'Variegatum' (variegated Solomon's seal) account for the majority of the square footage, while *Carex vulpinoidea* (fox sedge) and *Ageratina altissima* 'Chocolate' (chocolate snakeroot) fill the voids.

## Planting Palette for Ground-covering Perennials

Shade-tolerant plants listed here spread to form colonies with greater sociality due to stolons, rhizomes, or other space-occupying biomass. Species vary in their soil preferences but illustrate plant diversity of this archetype from across the globe.

*Pachysandra terminalis* (Japanese pachysandra) covers more acres outside of its native territory than it rightfully should when so many other groundcovers exist in so many more places. *Vancouveria hexandra* (inside-out flower), a relative of *Epimedium*, is a beautiful example with turgid, shiny leaves growing from a dense network of rhizomes just below the surface. In its native haunts in the moist understory below *Pseudotsuga menziesii* (Douglas fir), it forms dense colonies.

| PLANT NAME | GROWTH HABIT | ORIGIN |
|---|---|---|
| *Ajuga reptans* | Clump-forming/stoloniferous | Europe, Asia, and Africa |
| *Anemone canadensis* | Rhizomatous | North America |
| *Asarum* spp. and cultivars | Rhizomatous | Northern Hemisphere |
| *Carex blanda* | Clump-forming/rhizomatous | North America |
| *Carex divulsa* | Clump-forming/rhizomatous | Europe |
| *Carex pensylvanica* | Rhizomatous | Eastern North America |
| *Carex praegracilis* | Rhizomatous | Western North America |
| *Carex remota* | Clump-forming | Europe and Asia |
| *Carex woodii* | Rhizomatous | Eastern North America |
| *Chrysogonum virginianum* | Rhizomatous | Eastern North America |
| *Chrysosplenium* spp. | Stoloniferous | Northern Hemisphere |
| *Cornus canadensis* | Rhizomatous | North America |
| *Dennstaedtia punctilobula* | Rhizomatous | Eastern North America |
| *Epimedium* spp. and cultivars | Clump-forming/rhizomatous | Asia |
| *Eurybia divaricata* | Rhizomatous | Eastern North America |
| *Festuca subverticillata* | Rhizomatous | North America |
| *Fragaria* spp. and cultivars | Stoloniferous | Cosmopolitan |
| *Geranium macrorrhizum* | Rhizomatous | Europe |
| *Geum fragarioides* | Stoloniferous | Eastern North America |
| *Luzula* spp. | Rhizomatous | North America and Europe |
| *Maianthemum stellatum* | Rhizomatous | North America |
| *Mitella diphylla* | Clump-forming | Eastern North America |
| *Onoclea sensibilis* | Rhizomatous | North America |
| *Oxalis oregana* | Rhizomatous | Western North America |
| *Prunella vulgaris* | Clump-forming/stoloniferous | Cosmopolitan |
| *Ranunculus repens* | Stoloniferous | Europe and Asia |
| *Symphytum azureum, grandiflorum* | Rhizomatous | Europe |
| *Tellima grandiflora* | Clump-forming/stoloniferous | Western North America |
| *Tiarella cordifolia* | Clump-forming/stoloniferous | North America |
| *Vancouveria hexandra* | Rhizomatous | Western North America |

(TOP) While not the showiest garden plant, *Diarrhena obovata* (beakgrass) tolerates heavy shade in wet or dry soils where it holds a competitive advantage over most other plants that would fail on account of exposure or soil moisture. It can retain its greenness well into early winter and serves as an important winter food supply for game birds.

(RIGHT) *Oxalis oregana* (redwood sorrel) spreads both vegetatively and from seed to form extensive colonies in cool woodland conditions.

# THE NATURE OF GROWING

For all the commencement this book celebrates, most ecological gardening that any of us can do is still ahead. Once you've begun a planting in the New Naturalism tradition, you likely will find few reasons to return to yesterday's gardening. It's not for haughtiness or pride; it just doesn't make sense. I've never met a gardener who willfully sought to undo the very beauty of the outdoors in which they spend so much time. Yet I've known many gardeners who didn't realize what was really beautiful about the outdoors in the first place, or who didn't accept that the seeming smallness of their actions could contribute to an outsized effect with negative consequences. I hope anyone who reads this book will glean an idea that might inspire them to think differently about the nature of gardening and their relationships with land. Maybe you'll share that thought with your neighbor and plant a little community through the transaction of dirt-inspired conversation. We ought to think more in the garden, even as gardening is also a reprieve from the deadlines, text messages, and digital demands on our life. While restorative and calming, gardening doesn't have to be aimless.

Throughout writing this book, I questioned whether I could say all I wanted to say on this topic in the word count allotted. I couldn't. But by bringing you along to this point, more of us can now dig deeper into the lives of plants and consider sites as places for planting with purpose. We can continue to plant creatively, celebrate the moment, and lean into the planting schemes that thrive steadfastly. This pursuit of remarkable horticultural vegetation in everyday places can be an ordinary cause. With simply a good trowel and passion, the beauty and pleasure derived from planting resiliently would seem to overwhelm the alternative.

Further, the palettes could go on forever and probably should. The options for planting are always greater than the money, time, or space you have to plant them all. I hope, despite their brevity, that the archetypes provide a basis for planting your own dreams of a wilder, more nature-tuned landscape. If a handful of people everywhere planned and planted a garden to yield more than simply what they wanted or could eat themselves, imagine what this would do for the dragonflies and bees and sparrows and hawks. Imagine what those creatures would do for the food chain, the other insects they might eat, the honey they might make, or the rodents they might kill. Imagine watching all of this out your back door, your garden suddenly a podium for nature's presentations.

Imagine most of all a world with more plants that we've taken notice of. Plants run the world and look pretty good doing it. We don't have to personally covet them all, but we should want abundance, the mothering force of ecology even if it's not gregarious or seen. Abundance is captivating and enthralling, the kind of experience that our brains struggle to make sense of instead defaulting to awe, a feeling of reverence and wonderment. What if more gardens, no matter their size, struck people with awe? I hope you'll plant one and find out.

# ABOUT THE AUTHOR

**Kelly D. Norris** is an award-winning author and plantsman, and the director of horticulture and education at the Greater Des Moines Botanical Garden, a revitalized public garden in Des Moines, Iowa. Over his career, his work has been featured in *The New York Times*, *Organic Gardening*, *Better Homes and Gardens*, *Martha Stewart Living*, *Garden Design*, and in numerous local and regional media appearances. In 2019, Kelly joined Cottage Farms Plants on QVC as a guest host.

As a writer and photographer, he regularly contributes to popular gardening magazines like *Country Gardens*, *Fine Gardening*, *The American Gardener*, and a variety of industry trade publications. As a speaker, he has garnered acclaim for his high-energy, zealous presentations on the national stage, leading many to call him one of the rising stars of American horticulture.

Kelly has been fortunate to earn recognition for his work from a variety of organizations including three awards from Iowa State Horticultural Society (2009–2011) for his service and contributions to horticulture in Iowa; early career and young professional awards from the Perennial Plant Association (2011), GardenComm (2018), and the American Horticultural Society (2018); the Iowa Author Award for Special Interest Writing (2013), the youngest Iowan to be recognized in the history of the awards program; and a fellowship from the Chanticleer Foundation (2015) for his curatorial and plant exploration work at the Botanical Garden.

# INDEX

Abundance, ecological, 42, 50, 78–82, 204
Adam's needle, *91*
*Agave, 18, 38,* 169
Alliums, *58,* 70, 74–75, *85, 92–93, 98–99,*
 *110, 132, 136, 162,* 168
*American Eden* (Graham), 178
American goldenrod, *79*
Animals. *See also* Invertebrates; Mammals;
 Wildlife
 hedgerows and, 197
 plants coevolving with, 32
 understory and canopy supporting, 42, 50
Annual plants, 20, 111, 154, 160, *161,* 182.
 *See also* Reseeding annuals
Annual sunflower, 182
Arbuscular mycorrhizas, 14
Architecture, home, 46, 140
Architecture, plant, 16–20, 91, 96, 156
Asters, 17, *19, 30,* 32, 52–53, 116
Astible, *67,* 74–75, *83*
Azure aster, *19*

Baby's breath, 119
Bachelor's buttons, 21
Balkan sage, *155*
Bandera Helen's flower, *86*
Basal rosettes, 18, *18, 87, 125, 129,* 159, *170,*
 173, 191
Beachhead iris, 28
Beakgrass, 202
Beardtongue, *114–115, 127,* 144. *See also*
 Dark Towers beardtongue
Bee balm, 90
Bees, 50, 52, 134, 154
Big bluestem, 21, *21,* 40, 116
Biodiversity, *43,* 50, *51,* 52, 56, 167
Bioswales, 164
Birch trees, 187, *187*
Birds, 32, 33, 42, 63, 66, 126, 178
Bishop's flower, *94–95*
Bladder campion, *82*
Blake, Jimi, 70
Blake, June, 152
Blonde Ambition blue grama grass, *82,* 168
Bloodroot, *188*
Blue Fortune, *122*
Blue globe onion, *92–93, 132*
Blue sedge, *146*
Bog garden, 194–195
Borders, 156–161
Box elder, 42
Bridal Rice creeping willow, *124*
Brooklyn, NY courtyard garden, 150–151
Brown-eyed Susans, *40,* 53
Bulbs, plants grown from, 66
Bumblebees, 52
Bur oak tree, *190*
Bush honeysuckle, 169
Butterbur, 21
Butterfly weed, *51,* 53, *127*

C3 pathway, 23
C4 pathway, 23
Caespitose clumps/grasses, 19, 153, 159,
 173, 181
California poppy, *63, 106, 167*

Caradonna meadow sage, *152*
Cardinal beardtongue, *92–93*
Cardinal flower, *86, 92–93*
Case studies
 bog garden, 194–195
 courtyard garden, 150–151
 gravel and garden limestone wall
 planting, 174–175
 Roads Water-Smart Garden, Denver
 Botanic Gardens, 132–133
Cast iron plants, 188
Catmint, *82*
Chanticleer Garden, Wayne, PA, *187, 193*
Chasmophytic plants, 168, *177*
Chatto, Beth, 85
Citronella lily, *123*
Clay soil, 14, 53, 107, 161
Climate
 evaluating garden place and, 39
 plant adaptability and, 28–29
Climate change, 10, 29–30, 39, 52
Clover, 140
Clump-forming plants/architecture, 15, 19,
 *19,* 24, *25, 58, 59. See also* Caespitose
 clumps/grasses
Clumping grasses, *124,* 124–125
Coherence, 96
Colors, 96, 100
Columbines, 6, 21, *22, 23, 160*
Common black snakeroot, *190*
Common corn-flag, *70*
Common violet, *190*
Compacted soil, 12, 14, 41, 46, 102, 140, 161
Competition/competititveness, 20–21, 23,
 86–89, 90–91, 96
Compost, 41
Concrete edges, plantings for, 170–173
Coneflowers, 17, 23, *74–75,* 88, *97, 115,* 130
Container gardening, wild, 154–155
Contrast, planting for, 91, 96
Corabells, *72–73*
Courtyards, 146–153
Cranesbill, *57, 59,* 188, *193*
Crassulacean acid metabolism (CAM), 23
Creeping buttercup, 145
Creeping fig, *171*
Creeping juniper, 59
Creeping phlox, 17
Creeping woodsorrel, 154
Crinum lily, 76
Cultivars, 31–32, 50
Culver's root, *123*
Cup plants, 32, *56*
Curbside plantings, 178–183
Curry plant, 59
Cutleaf stephanandra, 59

Daffodils, *57,* 66
*Dahlia,* 17, 82
Daikon radishes, 161
Dandelions, 18, 140
Dappled conditions, *52. See also* Shade
Dark Towers beardtongue, *71, 86,* 203
Daylilies, 17
Deer, 32, 42, 56, 86
Dense blazing star, *25*

Dense plantings, 36, *56,* 101–104, 111, 132
Denver Botanic Gardens, *63, 132,* 132–133,
 *133, 180,* 182
Design, garden, 77–101
Dianthus, *127*
Diversity. *See also* Plant diversity
 species, 42, 142
 tree canopies and, 186–187
Drawings, 100
Drift planting pattern, 89–90
Driveway, residential planting along, *37*
Drumstick allium, *74–75, 85, 98–99*
Dunnett, Nigel, 126
Dutton, G.F., 96
Dwarf chestnut oak, 169
Dwarf goatsbeard, *193*
Dwarf larkspur, *25*
Dwyer, Mark, 161

Eastern horsemint, *193*
Ecoregions, 28
Ecotypes, 53
Edges, of a planting, 104
Edges, planting along, 170–173
Edible plants, in border garden, 161
Eischeid, Austin, *123*
Elm trees, 17
Emblematic plants, 66, 70, 113
Emergent stems, 19
Epping, Jeff, *58, 118, 127*

False hemp, 76, *76*
False indigo, 6, 16
Fernleaf yarrow, *87*
Ferns, *18,* 20, *61, 172, 177,* 188
Fertilizer, 11
Fingerleaf rodgersia, *190*
Firetail mountain fleece, *72–73*
Fir trees, 16
Fleeceflower, *123*
Flowering tobacco, *106*
Flower show gardens, 36, *37*
Food crops, 12, 161
Form, plant, 63
Foundations, border gardens along,
 156–161
Foxglove, 17, *57*
Front yards, 141–145

Gambel oak, 169
Garden(s)
 cultivating wildness in, 10–11
 designing plant communities for, 77–101
 finding inspiration for your, 36–37
 layering plants in.*See* Layered typology
 maintenance, 107–111
 nature and, 6, 7, 9
 qualities of an ecological, 54–56
 restarting, 109
Garden cosmos, 21
Gardening. *See also* Planting(s)
 change in, 70, 101
 collector's mindset for, 56–57
 evaluating sites for, 37–46
 matching plants to place, 48–53
"Genius of place," 9

Geraniums, 19, *19, 134*. *See also* Cranesbill
Giant ironweed, *35*
Giant needle grass, *40*, 41
Gold Dew tufted hair grass, *83*
Golden, James, 150
Goldenrod, 78, *79*
Grace hybrid smoketree, *158*
Graham, Wade, 178
Grasses. *See also* Caespitose clumps/grasses;
    individual names of grasses
  in border gardens, 159
  clumping, for meadow and mixed
    plantings, 124–125
  as competitors, 21
  in open and exposed landscape, 115, 116,
    117, 119
  in "steppes" environment, 126
Grasslands, 41, 42, *55*
Gravel gardens, *85, 114–115*, 126, *130*,
    174–175
Gray birch tree, *186–187*
Great Dixter, *47, 184*
Green mulch, 36, 140
Grey Owl red cedars, *62*
Grime, J. Philip, 20
Groundcovering mats, 18
Ground-covering plants. *See also* Matrix
    layer
  planting palette for shade-tolerant,
    200–201
  for replacing lawns, 145
  in woodland floor, 198
Grubb, Peter, 105
Guinea Fowl dwarf goatsbeard, *152*

Hairy false goldenaster, *15*
Hairy melic grass, *125*
Hampton Court Flower Show, 36, *37*
Hansen, Richard, 24, 113
Hardscapes, 40, 166–185
  curbsides and hellstrips, 178–183
  matrix layer for, 169
  natural stone and concrete edges,
    170–177
  overview, 166–168
  plants growing in cracks of sidewalks,
    184–185
  structural layer for, 169
  vignettes for, 169
Heartleaf wood aster, 53
Hedges/hedgerow, 46, 140, 197
Hellstrips, 167, 169, 180–183
Herbaceous plants/plantings
  for hellstrips, 181
  in matrix layer, 59
  in open landscapes, 46, 116, 119, 121
  in shade/woodland settings, 189, 192
  in structure layer, 62, 63, 189
  for sunny and dry meadows, 129
  for wild-inspired borders, 158–159
Herbivores, 24, 32–33, 111
Heronswood Gold gooseneck loosestrife,
    *110*
*Hibiscus*, 66, *164*
Homes, gardens near, 138–165
  bioswales/rain gardens, 164–165
  borders, 156–163
  courtyards, 146–153

front yards, 141–145
matrix layer in, 140
overview, 138–140
structure layer in, 140–141
vignettes layer in, 141
wild container gardening, 154–155
Horizontal lines, contrasting vertical lines
  with, 96
Horsemint, *182, 193*
Horticultural layers. *See* Layered typology
Hunter, Leslie, 135

Indiangrass, 6, 21, *35*
Indigo bush, 6
Insects, 32–33, 42, 50, 52, 66, 178
International Code of Nomenclature for
  Cultivated Plants, 31
Invertebrates, 23, 30, 52, 109, 126, 134. *See
  also* Insects
Irises, 28, *60*, 66, *67*
Ironweed, *35, 56, 116*
Island beds, 156

Japanese anemone, 188
Japanese forest grass, *188*
Japanese iris, 67
Japanese pachysandra, *200*
Japanese primrose, 67
Jewels of Opar, *106*
Joe pye weeds, 32, 82, *164*
Junegrass, *177*
Juniper Level Botanic Garden, *177*

Keeled garlic, *168*
Kew Gardens, *74–75*
Kinnikinnick, 59, *177*
Kitschy plants, 76

Ladyslipper orchid, 76
Lampwick plant, 59
Larkspur, 21, *25, 114–115*, 187
Lavender, 17
Lawn(s)
  converting to a garden, 140
  groundcovers for replacing, *108*, 145
  reducing size/eliminating, 142
Layered typology. *See also* Planting palettes
  laying out a new planting and, 104
  matrix layer.*See* Matrix layer
  overview, 57–58
  planting redundantly within and among,
    78–82
  spreadsheet/table/lists accounting for
    plants in, 100–101
  structure layer.*See* Structure layer
  vignettes layer.*See* Vignettes layer
Leafy mounds, 19, *135, 193*
Legibility, 96, 111
Legible frames, organizing garden around,
  46, *47,* 58, 96, 116, 156
Le Roy, Luis, 101
Light
  for open landscapes, 114–115
  site analysis and, 41
Lilyturf, 59
Limestone, 168, 174–175
Lists, of planting choices, 100–101
Lithophytes, 168

Little bluestem, *118, 124, 203*
Lloyd, Christopher, *47,* 108
Longevity, plant, 17, 20
Long Look Prairie, *38,* 40, *54–55*
Loosestrife, 90, *110*
Louisiana sage, *27,* 182, *182*
Lurie Garden, Chicago, IL, *88*
Lydian broom, 59

Magnolia trees, 188
Maltese cross, *125*
Mammals, 32, 33, 42, 50, 126, 178
Maple trees, 16, 188
Masses, plants growing in, 90–91
Massey, John, 155
Matrix layer, 58, *60, 61*
  about, 59–60
  bog garden, 194
  characteristics of plants in, 87
  courtyard gardens, 49, 151, 153
  at Denver Botanic Gardens, 133
  front yards, 142
  for gardens close to home, 140
  for gravel garden and limestone wall
    planting, 174–175
  for green shade, 189
  for hardscapes, 169
  for hellstrips in open exposures, 181
  for natural stone and concrete edges, 173
  in open landscapes, 117, 119
  remodeling a garden and, 100
  rose garden, 135
  species abundance in, 82
  for sunny and mesic conditions, 121
  for the understory, 191
  wild-inspired borders, 159
Meadow buttercup, 70
Meadow cranesbill, 57
Meadow Nord, *8*
Meadow rue, *90,* 119
Meadows, *22, 27,* 39, *115–116,* 119, *141, 144*
  clumping grasses for, 124–125
  planting palette for sunny and dry,
    128–129
Meadowsweet, 42
Mead's milkweed, 6
Mesic/moist conditions, planting palette for
  sunny and, 120–121
Mexican feather grass, *63, 85, 114–115,
  132, 193*
Mexican lily, *176*
Michigan's lily, 48, *49*
Milkweed, 6, *51,* 53
Miss Willmott's ghost, 87
Mondo grass, 140
Monoculture, 15, 41, 82, 90, 140
Moorgrass, 59, *86, 105,* 164
Moss, *177*
Moths, 154
Mount Everest ornamental onion, *110*
Mulch(ing), 59, 60, 102–103, 164
Mullein, 17, *44–45, 76–77*

Nagoya golden lace, *72–73*
Narcissus "Stint," *71*
Native plants
  benefits of using, 30
  building gardens from, 50

defining "native" and, 29
plant diversity and, 50, 52
Native seeds, 106
Natural stone, planting along, 170–177
Nature, gardening and, 6, 7, 9, 36, 55, 203–204
"Near-native" plants, 30, 50
Nettle-leaved mullein, *74–75*
New York ironweed, *56*
New Zealand hair sedge, *155*
Nonnative plants, 29, 50, 52, 150, *190, 193*
Nutrients, soil, 12, 13–14

Oak trees, 17, *40, 51,* 169, 187, *188*
Olmsted, Frederick Law, 9, 40–41, 189
Open landscapes, 114–137
clumping grasses for meadow and mixed plantings, 124–125
herbaceous-dominated planting schemes, 46
matrix layer in, 117
overview, 114–116
painting palette for sunny and mesic conditions, 120–123
Roads Water-Smart Garden, Denver Botanic Garden, 132–133
rose gardens, 134–137
steppe-inspired garden, 126–129
structure layer in, 63, 117
sunny and herbaceous, 119–123
vignettes in, 117–118
weeds, 131
Orange-flowered groundsel, *28*
Orange-flowered milkweeds, 53
Organic matter
hardscapes and, 168
healthy soil and, 13, 14
plant diversity and, 111
preparing for planting and, 102
restarting a garden and, 109
in steppe-inspired gardens, 126
Organic mulches, 102
Oudolf, Piet, *74–75,* 90
Oxeye daisy, *57*

Pale Indian plantain, *122*
Palettes. *See* Planting palettes
The Pearl sneezewort, *87*
Penstemon "Dark Towers," *71, 86, 203*
Peonies, 17
*Perennials the Their Garden Habitats* (Hansen and Stahl), 24, 113
Phenotypes, cultivars and, 31–32
Phlox, *87, 187, 190*
Photosynthesis, 23
Pine trees, 16, *16*
Pink muhly, 66, *68–69, 74–75*
Place(s)
considering how you will use your garden and, 42–43, 46
curating plants and, 56–57
evaluating sites to achieve a sense of, 37–42
matching plants to, 48–53
planting with a sense of, 34–35
size of garden/yard and, 36
Plant(s). *See also* Annual plants; Ground-covering plants; Herbaceous plants/plantings; Native plants

kitschy, 76
layering. *See* Layered typology
matching to place, 48–53
in matrix layer. *See* Matrix layer
social lives of, 24, 26, 28–33
soil's impact on, 14–16
structural. *See* Structure layer
survival strategies, 20–23
in vignettes layer. *See* Vignettes layer
woody, 16, 18, 50, 59, 62, 117, 143, 149, 153
Plant architecture, 16–20, 91, 96, 156
Plant communities
assembling/designing, 77–101
drifts of naturalized color in, 89–90
plants sharing common evolutionary heritage in, 78
Plant diversity, 50, 52, 78, *80–81,* 82, 89, 108, 111, 119
Planting(s)
act of, 103–104
contrast and, 91, 96
cultivating density and synergy in, 101–102
drift planting pattern, 89–90
ecologically compatible, 82–89
establishing a new, 104–107
monocultural blocks in, 90
power of 10, *91*
with a sense of place, 34–35, 53
site preparation for, 102–103
using both plants and seeds to establish, 105–107
wilder gardens, 6–7
Planting palettes
about, 113
for bog garden, 194
for courtyards with shady exposures, 148–151
for courtyards with sunny exposures, 152–153
Denver Botanic Gardens, 132–133
for front yards, 142–145
for groundcovering perennials, 200–201
for hellstrips in open exposures, 180–181
for natural stone and concrete edges, 172–175
rose garden, 134–135
steppe-inspired gardens, 126–131
for sunny and dry meadows, 128–129
for sunny and herbaceous gardens, 119–125
for sunny and mesic conditions, 120–121
for understory, 191–192
for wild-inspired borders, 158–159
Planting plans, 46
Plant metabolism, 23
Plant origins, 28–32, 50
Plant population, 24
Plant survival, 20–23
Plugs, 103
Plume poppy, *158*
Pocahontas beardtongue, *144, 162*
Poker plant, *90*
Pokeweed, 76
Pollinators, 32, 52
Pope, Alexander, 6
Poplar trees, 17
Populations, plant, 24–26

Power of 10 planting, *91*
Prairie blazing star, *79, 118*
Prairie dropseed, *58, 59, 86, 124, 168, 203*
Prairies, 6, 115, 119. *See also* Long Look Prairie
Prairie spiderwort, 6
Precipitation, 39
Princess tree, 21
Productivity, 14–15, 20
Protozoas, 14
Pruning, 17
Purple coneflower, 23, *74–75, 88, 114–115*
Purple lovegrass, *51, 91, 144, 179*
Purple osier willow, 42
Purple Rain, *70*
Purple Sensation, *162*
Purpletop, *94–95,* 106, *137*
Purrisan Blue catmint, *82*
Pussytoes, 18

Radishes, 161
Rain gardens, 164
Rattlesnake master, *88*
Redbud tree, 169
Redundancy, 78, 88–89
Redwood sorrel, *202*
Regeneration niche, 105
Reptiles, 42
Reseeding, 17–18, *22,* 23, 107
Reseeding annuals, *96,* 106, 135, 175
Residential neighborhoods/streets, 36, 182, *183. See also* Homes, gardens near
Restarting the garden, 109
Rhizomes, 17, 21, 24, 59, 111, 200
Roadside wildflowers, *168*
Rock clematis, *177*
Roots, function of, 16
Rose gardens, 134–137
Rose mallow, 164
Royal fern, 17
Ruderality, 70, *168,* 169
Ruderals, 20, 21, 23, *63, 82, 86,* 88, *96, 106,* 107, *160, 182*
Russian sage, *118,* 126, *158*

Sand lovegrass, *82*
Sandy soils, 53, 107
Sawsepal beardtongue, *177*
Schilling spurge, *90*
Sea kale, 21, *168*
Seasonal themes and interest, 100
Sedge, *19,* 59, *61,* 78, *86,* 108, 140, *146, 154, 155, 179, 190, 193*
Sedum, 59, *170*
Seed(s)
establishing plantings from, 105–107
native, 106
weed, 109
Seedbanks, 104–105, 107, 140
Self-heal, *61, 82*
Self-sowing plants, 59, 105, 107
Sensitive fern, *61, 199*
Shade
bog garden in, 194–195
ground-covering plants, 198–202
matrix layer for, 189
planting palette for an understory, 191–192

Shade, *continued*
planting palette for courtyards with, 148–149
structural layer for, 189
trees and, 186–188
understory, 189–193
understory trees for residential plantings, 195
vignettes layer for, 189
Shagbark hickory tree, *190*
Shrub canopies, 16
Shrubs
for edges and hedges, 197
lifespan of, 17
in matrix layer, 59
native, 50
in open landscapes, 116
plant architecture and, 16–17
Sidewalks, plants growing in cracks of, 184–185
Silk Road Orientpet lily, *158*
Silky fountaingrass, *85*
Site analysis, 39–42
Site, preparing for planting, 102–103
Sketched planting plans, 46
Small gardens
abundance in, 82
courtyards, 146–153
fine-scaled textures in, 119
plant diversity in, 82
random planting in, 101
Small plants, planting, 103
Smoketrees, 16, *127*
Sneezeweed, *97, 120*
Snow-on-the mountain, 182
Soil, 12–15, 102–103
Soil test(s), 13, 41
Spacing, of planting, 104
Spanish bluebells, *61, 182*
Species abundance, 78–82
Species diversity, 42, 142
Spencer, Tony, 83
Spiderwort, 6, *82*
Spreadsheet, of planting choices, 100–101
Sprengel's sedge, *61*
Spring-flowering bulbs/plants, *85,* 172, 173
Spruce trees, 16
Stahl, Friedrich, 24, 113
Star of Persia, *85*
Starry onion, *168*
Stemless four-nerve daisy, 21
Stemless gentian, 21
Stiff spurge, *182*
St. John's wort, *51*
Stolons, 21, 24, 59, 200
Stonecrop, 59
Stone edges/natural stone, plantings along, 170–177
Streetscapes (curbside gardens), 169, 178–183
Stressful environments, 59, 86–88, 102–103
Stress tolerators, 20, 21
Structure layer, 58
about, 62–63
bog garden, 194
characteristics of plants in, 87
courtyard gardens, 149, 151, 153

at Denver Botanic Gardens, 133
front yards, 143
in gardens close to home, 140–141
gravel garden and limestone wall planting, 174–175
for green shade, 189
for hardscapes, 169
for hellstrips in open spaces, 181
for natural stone and concrete edges, 172–173
in open landscapes, 117
planting palette for, 192
remodeling a garden and, 100
species abundance in, 82
for sunny and mesic conditions, 121
for wild-inspired borders, 159
Suan Unyamanee garden, Thailand, *64–65*
Succession, 26, 28, *63,* 66, 108
Sumac, 16, *17, 63*
Summer Beauty ornamental onion, *58*
Sun exposure, 114–115
Sunny conditions. *See also* Open landscapes
organic mulches in, 102
planting palette for courtyards with, 152–153
planting palette for wild-inspired borders with, 158–159
Switchgrass, 40, 119

Tanna burnet, *152*
Terraces, 146, 167
Texture, plant, 63, *92–93*
Tickseed, *116, 127*
Tillage, 102–103
Tillage radishes, 161, *162*
Trailblazer blazing star, *51*
Tree(s)
ecological profiles of, 16
lifespan of, 17
native, 50
observing your site and, 41
plant architecture and, 16–17
selection of, for planting, 186–188
taking down, 40
understory trees for residential plantings, 196
Tree canopies, 16, 40, 41, 42, 186–188. *See also* Understory
Tufted hair grass, 41, *83,* 119
Tulips, *38,* 66, *172, 191*
Turfgrasses, 141–142. *See also* Lawn(s)

Umbels, *94, 136*
Understory, 40, 146, 188, 189–193
Understory trees, 196
Urban areas. *See also* Hardscapes; Small gardens
bioswales (rain gardens) in, 164–165
ecotypes in, 53
soil in, 12, 140
tree canopies in, 41

Veitch's Blue globe thistle, *19*
Verticality, *98–99*
Vignettes layer, 58, *72–73*
about, 66–70
for bog garden, 194

characteristics of plants in, 87
for courtyard gardens, 149, 151, 153
Denver Botanic Gardens, 133
in front yards, 143
for gardens close to home, 141
for gravel garden and limestone wall planting, 174–175
for green shade, 189
for hardscapes, 169
for hellstrips in open spaces, 181
for natural stone and concrete edges, 172–173
open landscapes, 117
remodeling a garden and, 100
rose garden, 135
species abundance in, 82
sunny and mesic conditions, 121
for the understory, 192
wild-inspired borders, 159

Walek, Kristl, 106
Water, in the garden, 32, *33*
Waterperry Gardens, *87*
Weber, Scott, 183
Weed(s) and weeding, 102–103, 109, 111
Weeping brown sedge, *19*
Western sword fern, *18*
White bouquet tansy, *147*
White indigo, 6
White oak tree, *40*
Whorled milkweed, *51*
Wild bergamot, *27*
Wild columbine, 6
Wild container gardening, 154–155
Wild indigo, 17
Wild larkspur, *186–187*
Wildlife
attracting, 42
tree canopies and diversity of, 186–187
water in your garden for, 32
Wild petunia, *58*
Wild quinine, *118*
Williams, Kevin, 180
Willows, 17, 42, 63, 188
Windflower, 66
Wire vine, 59
Witchhazel, 169
Wolong Ghost, *172*
Wood ferns, 188
Woodland phlox, *186–187, 190*
Woodland pinkroot, *193*
Woodlands/woodland edge environment, 39, 42, *52,* 62–63, 102, 103, 109, 141, 186–202
Wood lily, 48
Woody plants, 16, 18, 50, 59, 62, 117, 143, 149, 153
Woolly groundsel, *28*

Xeric environment, 87, 109, 132
Xeric palette, *180*

Yellow coneflower, *92–93, 130*
Yucca, *63, 91,* 169